China in Progress

Preface

Since China's reform and opening up in 1978, China has advanced by leaps and bounds. Author had the opportunity to watch some reports about China on CCTV (China Central Television)*. Author found China's progress is comprehensive. It is amazing that its people were able to get out of poverty at end of 2020. China is constantly working on construction and improvement, and people's lives have greatly improved. In many areas, China has reached the world level, and in many areas, China is the world leader. China's progress has not been reported much. The purpose of this book is to report China's progress in detail.

*中国经济大讲堂- 12/20/2018-7/17/2022; 开讲了- 2/27/2016-7/30/2022

Frank Chi-Liang Yu   May 15, 2022, Missouri City, Texas, USA

Notes:

1. This book's ISBN numbers are ISBN: 9798845972521
2. This book has copyright protection.
3. This book is owned and published by Ten Books, Inc.
4. Please forward any comment to this e-mail address- feiyugospel44@gmail.com.
5. Index is not provided for this book. Reader should use 'Table of Content' for this purpose.
6. Square brackets, [...], is used to explain the source of reference. Parentheses, (...), is used for general explanation.

Acknowledge

Author wants to thank God to let this book be written. He also wants to dedicate this book to his parents, Mr. Nai-Hsi Yu and Mrs. Sue-Fang Tsai.

Author's Background:

Frank Yu was born in China and grew up in Taiwan province, China. He has B.S. degree from Tunghai University (Taiwan, China; 1966), M.S degree from University of Massachusetts (1969), and Ph.D. degree from the University of Texas at Austin (1975); all in Chemical Engineering. His profession is process design. After retired in Jan. 2011, he spent time in ESL teaching, translation, and writing.

Table of Content

Chapter 1 Introduction

Since the reform and opening up of China in 1978, China has advanced by leaps and bounds. The speed of progress is astonishing, and China has made progress in all areas. In some areas, China is leading in the world. Over the past 40 years, China's progress has been unprecedented in world history.

The first 6 chapters of this book review China's progress over the past 40 years- Chapter 1 Introduction; Chapter 2 People's Life; Chapter 3 National Defense and Military; Chapter 4 Science and Technology; Chapter 5 Space/Ocean Exploration; Chapter 6 Defend the Homeland. Chapter 7 is The Prospect of China's Future.

I. Reform and Opening up

In December 1978, Deng Xiaoping became the leader of China, he adopted a capitalist market economy- allowing private enterprises to exist. His theory was that it doesn't matter a cat is white or black, as long as the cat can catch mice, it is a good cat. He put aside political theory and focus on practical problem-solving. This is Reform and Opening up. China has also adopted democratic centralism, where the state manages the economy and state affairs [1]. Today, 40 years later, China has become the second largest economy in the world and is still moving forward.

II. China's progress in various areas

In June 1959, Soviet Union withdrew all aid from China, and China began to become self-reliant. In October 1964, China had an atomic bomb; in June 1967, China had a hydrogen bomb; in 1968, Nanjing Yangtze River Bridge was built; in April 1970, China launched a satellite; in the 1970s, rice breeding was successfully made; in June 2006, Three Gorges Dam was completed; in July, Qinghai-Tibet Railway was opened to traffic; in September 2016, Tianyan (Eye of Sky) was completed; in October 2018, Hong Kong-Zhuhai-Macao Bridge was opened to traffic; China has become self-sufficient in food since 2007; at end of 2020, China eliminated poverty. Others: High-speed rail/shield machine/greening desert/C919 airliner/5G/ building islands in South China Sea/Beidou Navigation System/ space station/retrieving lunar soil/landing on Mars, etc. These accomplishments demonstrate the diligent and hard work of Chinese people. China is also developing business in Africa and the Belt and

Road regions.

III. Defend the Homeland

In 1950, China resisted US aggression at Korea peninsula, repelled US military force and keep North and South Korea bounded by the 38th latitude line. In June 1962, India invaded Tibet and was repelled by China. In March 1969, the Soviet Union invaded Zhenbao Island and was repelled by China. In February 1979, China repelled the invasion of Vietnam. In 1997, Hong Kong was returned to China. In 1999, Macau was returned to China.

Reference
中国经济大讲堂(China Economic Lecture Hall)- Website address (same for the rest contexts): 20210418 政府为什么要拿自己开刀？

Chapter 2 People's Life

In this chapter, we're going to discuss China's progress in the life of its people.

I. Law

China's Civil Code [2] was passed in May 2020 and implemented on January 1, 2021. The Civil Code has 7 sections- general provisions/ property rights/contracts/personality rights/marriage and family/ inheritance/tort liability/sub-provisions, with a total of 1260 articles. The Code took 5 codifications to complete- drafted in 1954 (1st codification), 1964 draft (2nd codification), 4th draft in 1982 (3rd codification, It is the basis for the General Civil Law formulated later). The draft civil law was reviewed in December 2002 (4th codification), and in October 2014 (5th codification). [1-0:0-1:15]* The Civil Code replaces the General Civil Law. It is rich in content and has Chinese characteristics. It is comparable to other codes in the world. The personality rights are the first in the world. Others: Identify family rights relations, adjust social relations, define the role of government, look at the future of mankind.
* See Reference 1, Video- from 0 second to 1 minute 15 seconds]- (same for the rest contexts). [1]

China's Civil Code will help China on the path of ruling by law.

Reference
1. 中国经济大讲堂- 20201227 @所有人，《民法典》来啦！
2. 中国的民法典 (China's Civil Code);
http://www.npc.gov.cn/npc/c30834/202006/75ba6483b8344591abd07917e1d25cc8.shtml
Others:开讲了 (Voice- same for the rest of contexts)-
20190119 中国首位WTO上诉机构大法官，张月姣：为国际的和平正义作...

II. Cultural exchange

Through cultural exchanges, China will let other countries know her, and China will also know other countries.

Reference 中国经济大讲堂- 20191010 再塑经典，向世界讲好中国故事;
20190926 从再塑经典中展现文化自信

III. Protect traditional culture

China is modernized but has not forgotten to protect traditional rural culture.

Reference 中国经济大讲堂- 20210221 如何保护传统村落留住乡愁？

Commercial Press It was established in 1897, with the purpose of rejuvenating the country through education/strengthening the country with culture/serving the country with academia- prosperous education and enlightenment of people's wisdom. In January 1932, Japanese invaders bombed Shanghai, and Commercial Press was one of the four major targets, but Commercial Press has survived to this day and continues its original purpose.

Reference 开讲了- 20171230 商务印书馆总经理于殿利：建立文化强国
Other: 中国经济大讲堂- 20210124 数字技术如何留住千年敦煌石窟？；
20190711 如何破解中国古建筑的文化密码？；20220612 工业遗产如何活起来？；
20211024 探源中华文明：我们如何延续至今？；
开讲了- 20190907 "南海一号"保护发掘项目领队孙键：帆过浪有痕；
20181231 浙江省文物考古研究所所长，良渚古城的发现刘斌：中华五千年...；
20210116 本期演讲者：徐俊 history book; 20210206 本期演讲者：李守奎 Chinese;
20210216 本期演讲者：彭家鹏 Chinese music; 20210220 本期演讲者：王仁湘 food

IV. Education

Now is an era of the fourth industrial revolution*, characterized by society leading universities moving forward/multidisciplinary integration. University education needs to adapt to changes in talent needs, cultivate interdisciplinary talents, and deeply understand the connotation of innovation. University education needs to educate students about human values- mutual assistance, needs of the country- technology/major needs/economic development/people's life and health/society and people's needs; cooperation with society to cultivate talents/solve problems. [1]* Industrial Revolution: 1st one- invention of steam engine (1769), 2nd one- discovery of electromagnetic effect, leading to invention of electric motor and generator (1831), 3rd one- computer/internet/semiconductor (20th century), 4th one- IoT/AI/robotics (21st century) [2]

Reference 1. 中国经济大讲堂- 20201122 如何立足未来办教育？
2. 知乎- 第四次工业革命什么样?; https://zhuanlan.zhihu.com/p/96127474

The education in the information age will be student-centered/share the teaching of well-known teachers/use data to understand the situation of students' learning; the effect of teachers' teaching- provide support/focus on ability training/combination of human and technology- artificial intelligence to help teaching, allowing teachers to have more time to guide student. [11:43-38:19]

Reference 中国经济大讲堂- 20191130 信息技术如何"翻转"课堂？

Vocational school In China, parents want their children to go to regular high school*, not vocational school*, because they feel that graduating from regular high school is more promising. [0:0-12:41] This is due to parents' misunderstanding of vocational school. In fact, current vocational school not only train blue-collar worker, but also white-collar worker. Many vocational school graduates are operating machine, no manual work. * High school level- After graduating from junior high school, usually after passing senior high school entrance examination, student can choose these two types of high school to continue education. [12:41-19:27]

Now, those with high scores in senior high school entrance examination mostly choose to go to regular high school. In fact, the choice of which kind of high school should be decided according to personal interests/talents- those who are interested in management/ hands-on should choose to go to vocational school. [19:27-30:33] Vocational schools and regular high schools are cultivating two different kinds of talents. Vocational school must have their own teaching method and do not need to copy regular high school. Vocational school should be linked to the market/enterprise to allow students to gain practical experience. [30:33-41:08]

Reference 中国经济大讲堂- 20220102 如何让职业教育未来变得更香？

Review of a Shenzhen University alumni Shenzhen went from barren to a modern city. His own changes- experienced land reclamation in Shenzhen- engaged in internet reclamation- participated in public welfare undertakings.

Reference 开讲了-20180428 陈一丹开讲：做新时代"开荒牛"，开拓创新砥砺前行

Other: 开讲了-20180519 西安交通大学教授，国际数值传热学知名专家陶文铨院士：我是…
20171202 中国音乐学院院长王黎光：坚定文化自信，建立中国的音乐学院；
20170916 著名结构生物学家施一公：知足常乐是创新的大敌；
20160423 陈履生：每个人都应该走进博物馆；20200829 本期演讲者：朱永新 zoom

V. Agriculture

Rice It has been produced in China for more than 8,000 years, and 60% of Chinese staple food is rice. After the Opium War, China's lack of food self-sufficiency was a problem. After the founding of

New China (1949), grain production was better, but only 200-300 jin (1 jin = 0.5 kg) per mu because of poor varieties and no fertilizer. (mu is Chinese land unit, 1 mu=0.16 acre) [1-8:28-9:25] Raising the level of grain production depends on science and technology- selecting superior varieties and production techniques (fertilization, pesticides, etc.), in the 1970s, China had hybrid rice, and in the 1980s, China had chemical fertilizer. The yield of rice per mu has reached to 400 kg*, and some can reach 1000-1200 kg. Food issues are improved. [1-11:40-12:50] Now, China is starting to pay attention to improving the quality of rice- taste/nutrition/storage/ fertilizer absorption, etc. * General rice yield per mu- from over 300 kg in the 1980s to 470 kg in 2020. [1]

Reference 1. 《开讲啦》 20200718 本期演讲者：万建民
2. 开讲了- 20210807 本期演讲者：谢华安

Small science and technology institute Long-term large-scale use of chemical fertilizer is harmful to the land- soil will become acidic, hinder the growth of roots/prone to pests and diseases, etc.; rational use of chemical fertilizer will not be a problem. Agricultural experts are needed to guide farmer on how to farm. Since 2009, experts from agricultural schools in China have been stationed in rural areas- forming small science and technology institute to help farmer solve problems. Now, there are 263 small science and technology institutes across the country, covering 45 kinds of farming, more than 200 villages participated. [16:24-24:25]

Reference 《开讲啦》 20201017 本期演讲者：张福锁

Sea rice Sea rice (saline-tolerant rice) refers to a variety of rice that can grow in saline-alkali land with a salt (alkali) concentration of more than 0.3% and can produce more than 300 kg per mu.

In 1986, Chen Risheng (陈日胜), a researcher at Guangdong Ocean University, discovered the first wild sea rice on the coast of Zhanjiang (湛江), and applied for a patent for the new variety, named "Haidao 86". it was appraised by Academician Yuan Longping (袁隆平院士) as a breakthrough in rice industry after hybrid rice.

On January 15, 2021, Yuan Longping's sea rice team (袁隆平海水稻团队) announced at the 5th International Sea Rice Forum held in Sanya, Hainan (海南三亚) that it has signed a 6 million mu saline-alkali land renovation project across the country and will officially start industrialization and commercialization of sea rice in 2021. It is planned to achieve the goal of 100 million mu of saline-alkali land renovation and renovation in 8 to 10 years.

Reference 海水稻; https://baike.baidu.com/item/海水稻/15917703

Unmanned farm It is a farm without man. The production steps of farming, management and harvesting are all done by machines. For example, the 6 steps of rice production- tillage (ploughing)/planting/ field management (fertilization)/harvesting (threshing)/drying/straw processing can now be handled with Beidou Navigation System. Five features of unmanned farms- 1. Full coverage of cultivation management and harvesting, 2. Fully automatic operations between field and shop, 3. Ability to automatically avoid obstacles, 4. Ability to monitor the growth of crops, 5. Intelligent and accurate decision-making.

China started this research in 2001. In 2006, the first unmanned rice transplanter was successfully developed. Beidou navigation accelerated the realization of unmanned farms. In 2020, the first unmanned rice farm began. [11:26-25:00]

Reference 开讲了- 20201107 本期演讲者：罗锡文

Plant factory It started in Denmark in 1957. [2] Plants are planted in factory (non-natural environment- no land/sunlight), cultivated and harvested by human using technological method. The process is sowing-seedling-cultivation (nutrients are provided by sensor, provided by an intelligent control system), and LED lighting is used. Benefit- fewer workers, faster plant growth and more production*, working environment is comfortable and the work is not too hard. [1-0:30-2:35] China started to have plant factories in 2009. Plant factories can guarantee future food supplies. * A piece of lettuce usually takes about 70 days to grow, about 50 days for a greenhouse, and about 21-25 days for a plant factory; a plant factory can have 10 layers and can be produced throughout the year, production is 40-100 times that of ground plantation. [1-16:30-23:00]

Reference 1. 开讲了- 20200711 本期演讲者：杨其长
2. https://baike.baidu.com/item/植物工厂/3108283

China's agriculture China's annual production value of an agricultural labor force is 5,800 US dollars, while United States is more than 80,000 US dollars, so China still needs to work hard. Problem- China's farming population is declining, aging, low fertilizer/irrigation, losing money. China needs to develop agricultural technology to solve these problems.

Smart agriculture includes information perception/quantitative decision-making/intelligent control/personalized service, using scientific methods/machines to engage in crop growth/livestock raising/harvest/waste disposal. The characteristics are that it requires less labor/harvest and profit high. Beidou navigation will help the implementation of smart agriculture. China already has institutions to help farmers' production problems.

Characteristics of Chinese Agriculture- Except for the large area of farmland in Northeast China, the area of farmland in other areas is small; the management methods of these two areas are different. [1]

Now China is the world's largest importer of agricultural products*, with an import value of nearly 60 billion US dollars, so revitalization of agriculture is needed. The way to revitalize agriculture is to cultivate and discover more agricultural talents.
*After 2004, China has become an importer of agricultural products; the largest importer is soybean. [2]

China now has 200 million mu of arable land*, farmers use mobile phones to check the situation of farmland, using the land GIS and remote sensing technology; some mobile phone software, through artificial intelligence, can also help farmers to diagnose/manage field problems. This online/offline farmland management technology still needs to be popularized. [3-3:28-16:56] Artificial intelligence can help farmers solve loan problems/insurance/identify quality/ improvement varieties/reduce fertilizer, etc. [3-16:56-40:32]
* China's total arable land is 1.8 billion mu.

Reference 中国经济大讲堂 1. 20210620 数字技术如何让农民"慧"种田？
2. 20190228 乡村振兴，我们目前最缺的是什么？
3. 20220403 如何用数字技术打造智慧农业？

Mushroom kingdom There are 3 types of creatures on earth- animal, plant, and fungi. China began to develop agaric/mushroom in the late 1970s and has now become a mushroom kingdom.

Reference 开讲了- 20210410 本期演讲者：李玉 mushroom

Other: 中国经济大讲堂- 20210328 农业生产如何"虫口夺粮"？；
20210307 如何让"铁牛"自己种地？；20190404 新型职业农民，你愿意当吗？；
20201220 科学育种如何让我们吃得更好？；20210404 如何"闲"变"钱" 让农民致富？；
20210314 化肥，你真的了解吗？；20220410 如何阻击外来"生态杀手"？；
20210919 如何打好种业翻身仗？；20220717 餐桌上的大科技：如何守好大豆产业安全？
开讲了- 20210403 本期演讲者：赵春江 smart agriculture

VI. Rural revitalization

After the reform and opening up, China's land reform, centered on contracting production to household, improved social and economic development, and promoted marketization and township enterprises. By 2017, private enterprises had accounted for three-quarters of national income. In 2006, China abolished the agricultural tax- farmers do not need to pay tax. [3:56-9:32]

Some current shortcomings of rural revitalization: agriculture needs to be modernized/farmers' income is low/inadequate rural public services/inadequate supply system for urban-rural integrated development. [9:32-20:08] Development approach: priority development of agriculture and rural areas/new urbanization of urban-rural integration. Synchronization of four modernizations: synchronization of rural modernization/industrialization/ informatization/urbanization. Five major revitalizations: industry/ talent/culture/ecology/organization. [20:08-37:21]

Reference 中国经济大讲堂- 20181220 瞄准"6+1"，如何读懂乡村振兴"路线图"？
Other: 中国经济大讲堂- 20190411 如何"接二连三"推进乡村产业振兴？；
开讲了- 20180324 国家行政学院生态文明研究中心主任张孝德：新时代，我们该如...

Transforming countryside Human/animal manure and garbage disposal: Over 40 years, people's lives have improved, human/ animal manure and garbage have become one of the sources of environmental pollution. In 2010, rural waste was about the same as city; after 5 years, rural waste reached 150 million tons, 2.25 times that of city. Half is discharged into natural environment without treatment. [0:0-3:32]

In 1985, China started a poverty alleviation program and a rural infrastructure construction program. Thirty years later, more than 90% of the safe drinking water has been completed. In October 2017, at the 19th National Congress of the Communist Party of China, a three-year plan for the rural revitalization strategy was put forward, including toilet revolution/people's environment improvement/village infrastructure construction, which is a socio-economic transformation action. [3:32-8:19]

Animal manure treatment is one of the most successful areas of rural pollution control: Ministry of Agriculture has formulated plans and laws to control it. [8:19-17:45] The toilet revolution has new tricks according to local conditions. [17:45-29:26] Rural garbage classification, effectively dealt with garbage. [29:26-42:08]

China's countryside, with the efforts of government and people, has solved the problem of human/animal manure and garbage disposal, and made the countryside more beautiful and livable.

Reference 中国经济大讲堂- 20200927 怎样让乡村更美丽？

The problem of elderly care in rural area In general, an area is an aging area, if its elderly population over age 65 is more than 14%. In rural China, in 2017, the number of people over age 65 reached 15%. The reason is that more people move to city, and in the last 5-6 years, young people have taken their whole families to city, leaving their parents in the countryside. [0:0-6:23]

The problem of caring for the elderly in rural areas- high cost/weak rural infrastructure and social services/low income/many difficulties faced by township nursing homes- low income of nursing staff, old age, mostly female/elderly's many demands. [6:23-22:54]

Solving the problems of the rural elderly- helping them to be independent/care funded from salaries when they are young, insurance, government/senior organizations and community care/long term care/increase elderly income. [22:54-41:25]

Reference 中国经济大讲堂- 20200412 谁来照护农村老人的晚年生活？

Other: 中国经济大讲堂- 20200830 如何创新驱动打赢净土保卫战？；
20200726 碧水保卫战：水环境治理如何攻坚"质"胜？；

VII. Away from poverty

In November 2015, China decided to eliminate poverty, improve people's life, and gradually realize common rich. In 2018, production and living conditions in impoverished areas improved significantly, and problems that plagued the poor for many years, such as difficulty in traveling, drinking water, electricity, communication, education, medical treatment, etc., have been resolved.

By the end of 2020, China is out of poverty, which is 10 years early than the poverty relief goal set by the United Nations. [1]

The criteria for poverty alleviation are two: no worry about food/no worry about clothing, and three guarantees- guaranteed compulsory education/basic medical care/housing security. The first step is 6 precise- whom to support/project arrangement/use of fund/reach household/dispatching proper personnel to each village/effect of poverty alleviation. [4-8:30-9:35] The second step is 5 actions- develop business/relocation/ecological compensation/develop education/guarantee the bottom line. [4-9:35-10:05]

China's away from poverty can be seen from the average annual income of Chinese: 2,334¥ ($423) * in 1992, 7,942¥ ($959) in 2000, and 70,828¥ ($10,413) in 2020. [2]
* ¥- Chinese dollar, yuan. $- US dollar.

Experts have studied many countries' economic development. They found that when people's average annual income reaches 10,000 US dollars, its national economy stops developing. The nation that can continue to develop have a characteristic- its service industry is particularly developed. Experts suggest that China needs to rely on two methods to continue to increase the income of its citizen- reform and opening up and to introduce international competition and comprehensive technology/intelligence to promote the service industry. China has already done the first, for the second one- China has good foundation in 5G/internet/various technologies, so there is a good chance of success. [3]

Reference
1. 脱贫攻坚战; https://baike.baidu.com/item/脱贫攻坚战/18891455
2. 中国和美国人均收入相关指标比较一览（1992-2020）；
https://xueqiu.com/5296061618/210620337
中国经济大讲堂- 3. 20200307 新突破 新起点 未来如何迈向高收入阶段？
4. 20190704 脱贫攻坚，我们如何挑战不可能？

VIII. Industry

Engine In 2018, China's internal combustion engine output exceeded 80 million units, ranking first in the world for 8 consecutive years. Its technology has reached international standard, and production accounting for 1/3 of the international market. [0:0-6:27]

There are 5 indicators to evaluate an engine: high efficiency/low emission/high reliability/easy to operate/intelligent. Challenge- energy saving/protect environment/carbon neutral. [6:27-17:02]

China is a big engine manufacturing nation, but not a strong one, because lack of innovation of high-end products/lack of core parts manufacturing ability/lack in product quality stability. [17:02-27:57]

Needed development- government's innovation guidance/encourage innovation in enterprises/encourage research and innovation coordination from industry and academy/the service role of societies and industry associations. [27:57-39:26]

Reference 中国经济大讲堂- 20191114 动力升级，制造业如何打造强大的 "心脏"？

Chemical industry It is the backbone of national economy. The world's total chemical output value is 5.7 trillion US dollars, which is 7% of the total production value; chemical products are the basic raw materials, which will drive downstream products (1:4.2). China's total chemical output value is 12 trillion yuan, which is 40% of the world's output, and ranks first in the world. [6:33-11:27]

The traditional chemical industry uses petroleum/coal as raw materials, which has problems of pollution and safety. The latest development- biotechnology, which uses regenerated organisms as raw materials, greatly reduces pollution and safety issues. [11:27-23:12] In the next 10-20 years, chemical industry needs to use biotechnology and other technologies to solve other problems, such as the recycling of waste, which still needs efforts. [23:12-38:48]

Reference 中国经济大讲堂- 20191121 如何让化工更 "美丽"？

New energy vehicle There are 3 types: 1. Hybrid vehicle- the world started to have them in 1997. When the engine is inefficient, use electricity to drive, improve the efficiency of a car, 2. Battery electric vehicle- In 1992, the world had cars with lithium batteries, 3. Fuel cell electric vehicle - In 2015, the world had cars with fuel cells. Their features are having battery/motor/electronic control.

China needs to develop new energy vehicles, because it needs to save energy consumption/reduce pollution/upgrade the auto industry. China's auto industry: since 2009, its output has been the world's first (30%), China is a big nation of automobile, but not a strong one.

[5:49-21:48] It is estimated that electric vehicles will be widely used by 2035.

Reference 中国经济大讲堂- 20191031 补贴退坡，新能源汽车的未来在哪里？

High-quality development of manufacturing industry After 70 years of hard work, China's manufacturing industry is now a major source in the world*, but it is not a strong one, and efforts are still needed. * In 2010, China became the world's largest manufacturing nation. In 2017, China's manufacturing industry was 28.57% of the world's production. [4:34-13:31]

The goal of China's manufacturing industry: 3 steps- 2015-2025, after 10 years of hard work, to become the world's manufacturing powerhouse, another 10 years (by 2035) to become the world's top manufacturing powerhouse, another 10-15 years (by 2050) to become a leading power in the world's manufacturing industry. Key development areas: aerospace/information/transportation/power generation and transmission/ocean engineering/new energy vehicle/ robot/artificial intelligence/materials/agricultural machinery/ biomedical care/basic industries/greening environment/high-end equipment, etc. [13:31-26:38]

Measures to promote high-quality manufacturing: Actively promote the reform of manufacturing supply structure/improve innovation capability/talent supply/expand opening to the outside world/ improve the institutional environment. [20:38-41:47]

Reference 中国经济大讲堂- 20190314 制造业高质量发展难在哪？如何做？

IX. Energy Issues

Our world needs to reduce energy consumption and carbon emissions* to combat climate change. In 2014, China put forward the need for energy revolution/transformation- including production revolution/consumption revolution/scientific and technological revolution/system and mechanism revolution, to reduce fossil energy. The goal is that by 2030, non-fossil energy should reach 25% of total energy consumption, carbon emissions 65% lower than in 2005. [3:21-5:35] Non-fossil energy sources are mainly hydro/sun/wind. * Since 2006, annual carbon emissions of China are 5.5 billion tons, surpassed United States, and became the world's largest carbon emitter. In 2013, it reaches 100 billion tons. [5:35-7:00]

Reference 中国经济大讲堂- 20210509 能源新格局，“风光”如何担当重任？

Solving energy problem From 2000 to 2018, China's energy imports- 4.8% coal/> 65% oil/31.1% natural gas. [8:20] In order to solve the energy problem, China has made the following developments: 1. Using coal to produce petroleum and olefins* (important chemical raw materials) [8:20-16:00], 2. Reducing CO_2 emissions- research on how to use CO_2 to make useful chemicals, still in progress [17:06-25:30], 3. Using hydrogen as energy- fuel cell propulsion efficiency of hydrogen for electric motor is 60%, which is 200% higher than that of internal combustion engine, and no CO_2 emissions; still in progress- manufacturing/storage/cost issues need to be addressed. [26:48-40:00].
* Both products in China are at forefront of the world.

Reference 中国经济大讲堂- 20191228 破解能源危机的金钥匙是什么？

Hydrogen energy Hydrogen is non-toxic/clean/high combustion value, 1000 times that of wood, 6.8 times that of coal, 3.3 times that of gasoline, and 3.4 times that of natural gas. [3:30-5:26] The 21st century will be the era of hydrogen energy. The particularity of hydrogen energy: hydrogen energy generators do not generate heat, do not need a thermal cycle system, and the efficiency is as high as 90%/can reduce carbon emissions/a wide range of applications- deep-sea diving, drone, aviation, aerospace, home, etc./safe/no smog. [5:26-19:13] The use of hydrogen energy has started and will be more to come. [19:13-40:32]

Reference 中国经济大讲堂- 20190516 氢能如何改变我们的未来？

Wind/photovoltaic power It is a green renewable energy source. Their disadvantage is volatility- electricity can only be generated, when there is wind/sunshine. The core problem is that they require energy storage, thus raising their prices. Available energy storage methods are batteries/development of energy network/electric vehicles; battery safety still needs to be improved. The production cost of hydrogen energy is high, but the price of storage is low. Hydrogen energy can be complementary to wind/photovoltaic power generation. Thermal power plants can also use hydrogen to generate electricity, with the advantage of green and carbon reduction.

Reference 中国经济大讲堂- 20220619 减碳在行动：储存“风光”，路在何方？
Other: 中国经济大讲堂- 20220626 减碳在行动：盐湖“锂”的新能源密码；

氢燃料电池新能源汽车原理; https://zhuanlan.zhihu.com/p/76653046

Deliver gas from West to East From 2000 to 2007, China built a natural gas pipeline from Xinjiang to Shanghai; in 2009, a natural gas pipeline from Sichuan to Shanghai was built. The West-East gas pipeline is a major project after Three Gorges Dam. Gas pipeline construction work continues. [1, 2]

Reference 1. 西气东输; https://baike.baidu.com/item/西气东输/302708
2. 开讲了- 20170514 中石油管道设计院总工程师张文伟：能源管道串联世界
Other: 开讲了- 20210306 本期演讲者：金之钧 shale gas

X. Transportation

A major transportation nation In 2020, China has become a major transportation nation- in terms of number of high-speed railways/highways/inland shipping/urban rail transit/ports. China is the world's first. In terms of railway operation mileage/total road mileage/transportation airport, China is second in the world. [4:42] But China still is not a strong nation in transportation, because in terms of high-tech transportation equipment, there is still a lot of dependence on foreign countries/the level of transportation services is not high. [4:59-11:59] China needs to improve to become a transportation strong nation. It is estimated that it will take 10 years. [24:57-42:00]

Reference 中国经济大讲堂- 20200215 建设交通强国重点要做好哪些事？

XI. Transforming the environment

Climate change This is a global problem. From 1750 to 2020, the global temperature has risen by 1.2C. The current global temperature rise has accelerated- the 10 years of the warmest global temperature have occurred in the 21st century. [5:55-6:43] The result is warmer temperatures around the world/heavy rain or typhoon in some areas/rising coastline/droughts. [6:43-13:19]

Cause: There are natural and man-made causes. Man-made causes are mainly emission of greenhouse gases* and aerosols (gases or liquid particles floating in atmosphere). What we can control is man-made causes. Earth receives solar energy, and it also reflects energy; if the two are not in balance, earth will either heat up or cool. Greenhouse gases prevent earth from dissipating heat, causing its

temperature to rise; aerosols reflect the sun's energy, causing its temperature to drop. It is estimated that greenhouse gases have historically increased earth temperature by 1.5C and aerosols have decreased its temperature by 0.4C. [13:19-20:02]
* Such as CO2/methane/nitrous oxide. Before Industrial Revolution, the concentration of CO2 in the atmosphere was 180-280ppm. After Industrial Revolution, the concentration of CO2 continued to rise, reaching 413ppm in 2020.

Scientists have identified 9 tipping points to observe the catastrophes of global warming, such as Arctic ice/Amazon Forest, etc. [20:02-23:47] Climate warming is known to cause disasters to human life/health/environment; the main disaster for China is high temperature/heavy rainfall/drought. [23:47-34:28] Currently, the international forecast is that by 2040, the global temperature will rise 1.5C. Solution: reduce greenhouse gas emissions or reduce its concentration in the atmosphere; the former we can reduce the use of coal/oil and use renewable energy- such as hydro/sun/wind to generate electricity; the latter- such as plant more trees. Others: improved facilities to deal with floods/droughts, improved varieties to cope with high temperatures, etc. [34:28-40:19]

Reference 中国经济大讲堂- 20220424 如何给地球"降温"？

Dual carbon goal In April 2021, China pledged to peak carbon emissions by 2030 and neutralize carbon emissions by 2060. This is the dual carbon goal. The core work is to transform the production methods with high energy consumption/pollution/emissions to green/sustainable methods.

Reference 中国经济大讲堂- 20210606 "双碳"目标如何引发绿色转型大潮？
Other: 开讲了- 20211211 本期分享者：潘家华 peak/neutralize carbon emissions

Crack the PM2.5 dilemma

PM2.5 refers to tiny dust in air, less than 2.5 microns in diameter; it can be solid/liquid/gas; it may come from dust/coal combustion/ automobile exhaust/industrial emissions, etc; it will make air produces smog, harmful to health- such as asthma/lung cancer/death. [1] Its concentration in air is a measure of air quality.

Studies have shown that the concentration of PM2.5 in air decreases by 10 μg/m3, and the mortality rate can be reduced by 0.13%. In 2012, China stipulated PM2.5 as a standard for air quality. In

September 2013, China promulgated the Air Pollution Prevention Action Plan- to control coal combustion/reducing emissions. [2-4:40-13:10] After 5 years, PM2.5 emissions have decreased by 38%; coal power plant emissions are the lowest in the world. [2-13:10-24:18]

Beijing's PM2.5 pollution is mainly due to secondary pollution. Secondary pollution refers to air pollutants such as sulfur dioxide/nitrogen oxides/ammonia turning into inorganic particles or volatile organics turning into organic particles. [2-13:33]

In 2018, less than 50% of the cities in China met the PM2.5 standard, and just 50% of the cities met the PM10 standard. China's environmental pollution still needs to improve. The direction is to reduce the emissions of enterprises/vehicles and increase the use of renewable energy. [2-24:18:41:10]

Reference 1. What is PM2.5 and why does it matter; https://www.cleanairresources.com/resources/what-is-pm-2-point-5-and-why-does-it-matter 2. 中国经济大讲堂-20191024 如何破解PM2.5之困，打赢蓝天保卫战？

Shelter Forest Project China's experience: After the founding of New China (1949), there was a lot of deforestation to earn foreign exchange, but the natural ecology was destroyed. In the 1970s, many problems occurred, such as sandstorms in the north, etc. So, China launched the Three-North Shelter Forest Project to build a green Great Wall in the northwest/north/northeast to block sandstorms. This is the largest ecological project in the world, and the project started in 1979 and will be ended in 2050. [3:30-8:32] In 1998, large floods occurred in both the north and south of China. The reason was also massive deforestation to increase agricultural land- resulting in soil loss; so, a natural protection project was initiated. China realizes the importance of forests. [8:32-17:27]

Problems of afforestation in China: The forests planted in China are artificial forests- less species, easy to be destroyed, not as good as natural forests. China has also begun to pay attention to planting trees that resemble natural forests. [17:27-29:19]

Forests have a huge carbon storage capacity and can mitigate climate change. So, it is necessary to protect forests/actively create and expand green areas/emphasize forest sustainability. [29:19-40:54]

Reference 中国经济大讲堂- 20220123 绿色经济如何挖好森林这座“富矿”？

Ten-year fishing ban in Yangtze River On January 1, 2020, a ten-year fishing ban began at Yangtze River. [1] Reason: The river has problems such as excessive fishing/long-term dam building/sand dredging/pollution. Its ecological damage needs to be rehabilitated. [2-5:20-21:21] It is hoped to restore the ecology of Yangtze River to the 1950s. [2-21:21-29:20] Besides fishing ban, government also need to help fishermen to find new jobs. [2-29:20-41:17]

Reference

1. 长江十年禁渔计划; https://baike.baidu.com/item/长江十年禁渔计划/24242822
2. 中国经济大讲堂- 20210926 如何读懂长江十年禁渔？
Other: 开讲了-20200215 中科院水生生物研究所研究员刘仁俊：等待下一只白鱀豚出水一跃 20210821 本期演讲者：危起伟 Yangtze River

Governance of Yellow River Yellow River Basin gave birth to Chinese culture. Due to the increase in population, the forest land was reclaimed as farmland, causing the problem of soil loss. In the 1970s, the amount of sediment transported by Yellow River was 1.6 billion tons, making the land barren and people's life difficult. [9:12-13:34] Management of Yellow River- increase vegetation, in 2017, the sediment transport of Yellow River has dropped to 100 million tons. Yellow River has changed, and there have been fewer floods. Now, the vegetation of Yellow River Basin has reached 64%, double the previous area. [13:34-27:07] The work of protecting Yellow River is still going on.

Reference 开讲了- 20191130 黄河治理专家 刘国彬开讲：黄土情、黄河梦

Sanjiangyuan National Park It is in the southern part of Qinghai Province. Sanjiangyuan area is one of the birthplaces of Yellow River, Yangtze River, and Lancang River. Sanjiangyuan National Park is the largest national park in the world. After 40 years of hard work, it was completed in 2020 and construction continues.

Reference 开讲了- 20201003 本期演讲者：赵新全 - Sanjiangyuan National Park
Other: 三江源国家公园; https://baike.baidu.com/item/三江源国家公园/19508404#1_1

Saihanba It is in northern Hebei Province. Beginning in 1962, after 59 years of afforestation, the former high, arid, and desertified wasteland has been transformed into a forest of millions of acres. It was damaged by a natural disaster in October 1977, but the afforestation has continued to this day.

Reference 开讲了- 20210417 本期演讲者：陈智卿 Saihanba

XII. China's economy

Now, China's economy is in the middle-income stage. Before this, people pursued material life. In the 70s, the pursuit was to eat well, in the 80s, the pursuit of clothing, in the 90s, the pursuit of durable consumer goods- such as bicycles/refrigerators/TVs, etc., and then cars/houses. Now, an improvement in the quality of life has been pursued. To meet this need, the industrial structure needs to be transformed. It needs high technology and more skilled worker, and it will take longer to have them. The economic conditions of different regions in China are also different.

American economist Rostow believes that a country's economic development has two stages- traditional economy and modern economy. Traditional economy relies on natural resources (mainly agriculture); modern economy mainly relies on technological development (mainly service sector- 60-70% of the economy/over 90% of people live in cities). The transition from the traditional economy to the modern economy must go through a process of take-off (mainly manufacturing). China's economic take-off started in the 1990s; there are two characteristics- rapid development and changes in industrial structure. At present, China's service industry accounts for 50% of the economy and urban population is less than 60%, so China's economy is still at taking off stage.

Good reforms can boost the enthusiasm of producers and drive economic growth. The advantage of China's economic development is that China itself is a big market. [1]

The future development of China's economy depends on- developing the service industry/accelerating urbanization/innovating and integrating the manufacturing industry/promoting the Belt and Road business. How to unleash future economic potential- to further promote reform and opening up/cultivating talents/maintaining a stable international environment. [2]

Reference 中国经济大讲堂-
1. 20190103 坐稳扶好，中国经济如何完成"起飞"？（上）

The potential of China's economy The trade war between China and USA started in March 2018. China's exports to USA are 20% of total exports. How will this trade war affect the Chinese economy? [3:30-6:59] China has adopted tax and fee reductions to ease the burden on enterprises and activate the economy. [6:59-12:14]

The potential of developing China's economy from advantages and disparities: China's consumption market is huge/there is still a lot of room for infrastructure investment/urbanization is still accelerating/there is room for maneuver between regions/active technological innovation/young successors come/the gap with international is also potential for development. [12:14-28:01] What needs to do further is to deepen the reform of supply side/enhance the vitality of market entities- fair competition/improve the level of industrial chain/smooth domestic and foreign economic cycles/promote a new round of reforms- strengthen property rights and protection of intellectual property rights, continue to deepen the reform of scientific and technological system, deepen the reform of state-owned enterprises, continue to create fair conditions for the development of private enterprises, promote high-level development, and enable talents [28:01-39:27]

Reference 中国经济大讲堂- 20190606 如何多点发力释放中国经济的潜力？

The resilience of China's economy As follows: reform and opening up has accumulated rich experience for China's economy [4:57]/ this is one of the most dynamic economies in the world- China is the locomotive driving the global economy [6:56]/One Belt One Road expands economic cooperation between China and other countries [8:58]/innovation will provide continuous impetus for China's economic development- China has strong human resources [19:30]/multiple regional development exhibition will unleash economic potential [23:06]/the growing consumer market is the driving force for China's economic development [30:18]/a complete manufacturing system is the foundation of China's economy [32:22]/the combination of soft and hard infrastructure is the foundation of economic development. [34:26-40:29]

Reference 中国经济大讲堂- 20190530 为什么中国经济仍具有巨大韧性？

Future of China's economy China is now in a moderate growth stage- 6-6.5% growth rate, which is normal; compared with 2000, the real growth rate is 30%, and compared with 2010, the real growth rate is 11%. The new growth rate of China's economy is the first in the world, which shows the potential of China's economy. [4:32-9:33]

China currently has 400 million middle-income people and 1 billion low-income people. At the end of 2020, after China has completed poverty alleviation, the goal of China's economic development is to increase the middle-income group to 800-900 million people, 60% of the total population; to make the society relatively stable for a long time. [9:33-14:00]

Momentum for the stable development of China's economy: building metropolitan areas- activating the energy of urban and rural development/relaxing access, encouraging competition- improving efficiency in an all-round way/improving human resource of low-income people- narrowing income and distribution gap/upgrading consumption- productive and knowledge-intensive service industry has a bright future/technological innovation- seize the opportunity of this round of technological revolution/green development- to make the new development system more competitive. [14:00-40:36]

Reference 中国经济大讲堂- 20190822 目标6%至6.5%，稳增长未来靠什么？

China's private enterprises They provide the nation with 50% of tax revenue, 60% of production value, 70% of technological innovation, 80% of urban employment, and 90% of enterprises. Private enterprises have made great contribution to China's economic development. [4:20-8:15]

Difficulties faced by Chinese private enterprises: insufficient market demand- fierce competition, it is a market for consumer/low return on investment/difficult and expensive financing/heavy tax burden/ few officials do nothing to help/property rights aren't effectively protected/discrimination against ownership/new officials ignore old account/transformation and upgrading/environmental protection constraints. [8:15-20:01]

Reasons for the difficulty: time is changed- the shortage economy has become a surplus economy/consumption concepts have changed/ enterprise development methods have changed/factors of production have changed- costs have increased/the legal environment has changed- not relying on relationship, but relying on strength/market is changed- globalization/business model is changed- no longer able to push cost to consumer/development concept is changed-innovation, development, green, etc. [20:01-32:08]

Confidence in the development of private enterprises: there is huge room for development- huge domestic demand, China is developing, the middle income is increasing, etc./there are challenges in outside environment, but there are also opportunities/use multi-pronged approach to help private enterprises overcome difficulties- cut taxes and fees. [32:08-42:03]

Reference 中国经济大讲堂- 20190117 民营经济如何翻越"三座大山"？

County economy China's territorial structure has 5 levels-government/province/city/county/township. There are 2862 counties in China, land is 93% of the whole nation, population is more than 70%, and GDP is 56%. Among the top 100 counties in China, 66 are in Jiangsu/Zhejiang/Shandong province, and their industries are all developing very well. The rest of the counties, if they can develop well, it will have a great impact on China's economy. [5:05-16:08]

How to develop the county economy: 1. Make a long-term development plan, 2. Build up the county/town/village, 3. Optimize industrial structure and realize agricultural modernization, 4. Respect the interests of farmer, 5. Reform the management system. [16:08-40:37]

Reference 中国经济大讲堂- 20190321 承上启下，如何发掘"县城"的巨大潜力？

Price reform It is the key to the success of economic reform Before the reform and opening up (1978), China's price was decided by the government, and the economic policy was to focus on industry and less on agriculture. [4:00-12:17] After reform, price reform is the most difficult and riskiest one. It has 3 stages: 1. From 1978 reform to the establishment of socialist market economy system in 1992-raising the prices of agricultural products and opening up the prices of commodities, 2. 1992-2012- continued price reform, canceled food stamps, stabilized prices, and gradually entered the market to determine prices, 3. After 2012- fully determined prices by the market, government supervision. [12:17-31:45]

The task of price reform in the new era: continue price reform, improve market-determined prices, and government supervision. [31:45-41:32]

China's economic opening in the new era Five characteristics: From introducing foreign capital to paying equal attention to foreign investment and outbound investment- RMB* gradually becoming an international currency/from export-oriented to both export and import- aim for balance/simultaneous opening of inland and coastal areas/trade from goods to both goods and services/from adapting to world trade to participating in rulemaking. [5:10-18:10] *RMB- Renminbi (in Chinese); Chinese money system.

The task of economic opening in the new era: increasing imports is a long-term strategic goal- reducing international friction/expanding areas for foreign investment. [18:10-25:30] 5 conditions for opening up inland economic highlands: start from a big city/must be a transportation hub/having port-custom inspection service/have a large platform- a free trade zone or new area/have industries access to the international market.

World economy In the 20th and 21st centuries, the biggest economic change in the world is China. [3:25] Current world economy has 10 major contradictions: 1. Inequality between rich and poor- 197 countries in the world, the top 10 nations have 80% of the world's production value, the next 10 nations have 10%, and the remaining 177 nations have 10% [4:00], 2. The relationship between developed nations and developing nations- after the Second World War- the international system was established for developed nations; but now the production value of developing nations has reached 56%, so there is a contradiction [4: 55], 3. The conflict between the old and the new [5:50], 4. The global balance of payment- high debt [7:45], 5. The conflict between unilateralism and multilateralism [9:30], 6. The paradox between opening and closing [11:05], 7. The paradox between the physical and virtual economy- the two need to match [13:15], 8. The paradox between aging and social security [14: 35], 9. Competition and game between great powers [15:17], 10. Multicultural conflict [15:55].

Changes in the global economic pattern: international trade/ international manufacturing/global energy- will be surplus/global finance/economic development momentum and power source- is undergoing adjustment and change- after 2008, China has become the driving force of world economy. [18:39-32:55]

China's plan: to realize socialist modernization by 2035 and become a powerful modern socialist nation by 2050. China's economy will be extended by 4 cycles: strategic opportunity period/economic development period/manufacturing prosperity period/consumer's lifecycle period; towards 4 medium-high: economy/industry/ people's income/talents. Within 10 years, it will reach 4 100%: get out of poverty/social security/network coverage/green environment. [34:00-40:38]

Reference 中国经济大讲堂- 20190425 变局百年未有，中国经济如何有效应对？
Other: 中国经济大讲堂- 20201206 如何看待资本市场新格局？；
20201108 美元背后的财富与隐忧；20201025 "十三五" 我们收获了什么？；
20200111 管理教育如何解决好中国企业的痛点？；
20190829 粤港澳大湾区，如何成为全球新的经济增长极？；
20190815 如何精准施策，破解中小企业融资难题？；
20190509 如何建设现代金融，打通经济 "血脉" ？；
20190418 高质量发展呼唤怎样的企业？；20181227 减税降费之路该怎样走？；
20210530 老龄化加剧，养老金如何养好老？

Asia-Pacific regional economic partnership agreement In November 2020, 15 nations in the Asia-Pacific region signed the Regional Comprehensive Economic Partnership (RCEP) after eight years of negotiations, resulting in the world's largest free trade area. This is a high-level economic and trade agreement- modern/ comprehensive/high-quality/reciprocal. It brings opportunities and profits to the regional economy and can promote the global economy.

Reference 中国经济大讲堂- 20210117 世界最大自贸区诞生意味着什么？

20 years after China joined WTO* China continues to cut taxes/open import/facilitate foreign investment, etc. Result: The world benefits/China's economy develops rapidly. [3:32-21:39] The world's view of China: Some praise China, some discredit China. [21:39-39:00] Reasons for China's rapid economic development: It has the support of a strong government/implemented an open policy. [29:00-41:28] * China joined the World Trade Organization (WTO) on December 11, 2011.

Reference 中国经济大讲堂- 20220109 回望中国加入WTO二十年

Renminbi (RMB) It is Chinese money system. Renminbi officially became the universal currency on October 1, 2016. [11:20-12:45] Many countries have accepted RMB, but efforts are still needed.

China's manufacturing industry The World Bank reported in July 2019 that China's manufacturing industry has been the largest in the world for 10 years (since 2010). [4:00-5:25] Facing the future, service-oriented manufacturing is the key to opening the door to profitability for manufacturing- manufacturing should add service, because design and service are more profitable. [6:53-11:24] In the manufacturing process, add various services to increase profits.

The Belt and Road In 2013, China proposed the Belt and Road initiative, which has received responses from various countries*. In May 2017, the first International Cooperation Summit Forum was held in Beijing. Through Belt and Road cooperation, China's neighboring countries, such as Laos/Thailand, etc., their economy has made great progress; made 5 connections*. [1-0:0-13:15]
* The focus of Belt and Road work is five connections: policy communication/facility connectivity/unimpeded trade/financial integration/people-to-people. In 2016, 25 countries participated; 54 countries in 2017; 139 countries in 2019; 149 countries in 2022. [2-3:58-5:56]

Belt and Road is a new model of international cooperation; it is an inevitable choice for the sustainable development of China's economy. The core is peaceful cooperation/openness and inclusiveness/mutual learning/mutual benefit/co-construction/sharing. The goal is to build a community with a shared future for mankind, and construction must benefit people's livelihood/green/open/integrity/high quality. [2-5:56-41:13]

Foreign trade In 2018, world trade was in a downturn, and China and United States started a trade war. China has put forward a policy to stabilize foreign trade- greatly relaxing market access/creating a more favorable investment environment/strengthening intellectual property protection/actively expanding imports. [4:36-9:19] China has also implemented tax cuts and optimized trade procedures. One year after the Sino-US trade war, China's foreign trade and foreign investment have increased unabated. [9:19-19:14] The future of China's foreign trade needs to continue to improve, and it will get better. [19:14-39:41]

Reference 中国经济大讲堂- 20190919 新挑战，新策略，我国外贸该如何稳？

Other: 中国经济大讲堂- 20201004 要素市场化改革：数据到底有什么用？; 20200614 新挑战，新策略，我国外贸该如何稳？; 20200531 如何在高质量发展中开拓就业新机遇？/如何建设现代...; 20211212 百年启示：中国经济的未来机会; 20211128 自由贸易试验区的新使命; 20211114 走向共同富裕：如何实现共同富裕？

XIII. Medical

New development in Chinese Medicine

Manufacture of Chinese medicine is now automated. [1]
Source of Chinese medicine- using artificial planting, not rely on wild growth. Now, it is self-sufficient. [1]
Authenticity of Chinese medicine- There are 11,000 kinds of Chinese medicine. Now, DNA barcode identification system is used to identify its authenticity. [1]
Inheritance of Chinese medicine resources- established a Chinese medicine gene bank. [1]
The basic research of Chinese Medicine needs to be strengthened and the evaluation system needs to be established; modern technology is the key to unlock the treasure of Chinese Medicine. [1]

Uniform standards/going international- It took 6 years, and in 2019, there was a unified teaching material open to the public. [2]
Achievements in the modernization of Chinese medicine- The total output value increased from 20 billion yuan in 1996 to 800 billion yuan in 2017, an increase of more than 30 times. [2]

Signed agreements with 86 countries, established dozens of Chinese Medicine centers, and 200,000 Chinese Medicine clinics around the world- with hundreds of thousands of practitioners (mostly locals). Chinese Medicine is used in 183 countries.[2]

There are 6 medicines used in China during COVID-19; 5 of them are Chinese medicine, 1 of them is Western Medicine; more than 90% of patients were recovered using Chinese medicine. [3]
Reference
1. CCTV 中国经济大讲堂- 20200913 如何持续发掘传统中药库中的珍宝？

2. CCTV 中国经济大讲堂- 20200426 健康中国：中医药如何守正创新，走向世界？
3. CCTV 健康之路- 20200529 中医战疫传奇（上）

Magical stem cell Stem cells are characterized by 1. being able to replicate endlessly, helping us grow and developing/metabolizing, 2. being able to replicate into a specific cell. [4:00-6:16]

Stem cells arc divided into 3 categories: 1. Adult stem cell- stem cells that can generate body tissues, such as dermal stem cells that grow into skin; 2. Human embryonic stem cell- can develop into various tissues and organs of human body; 3. Fetal stem cell- can develop into a fetus. Human embryonic stem cells have the highest developmental potential, followed by fetal stem cells, and finally adult stem cells. The most difficult to obtain are human embryonic stem cells, the most accessible are adult stem cells, and fetal stem cells are banned from use/research in many countries. [6:16-10:04]

In 2018, China successfully developed non-embryonic stem cells (without fertilization) into a small mouse. [13:22-19:57] In 2015, China began to use stem cells to treat diseases. [19:57-27:43] The application of stem cells to create various tissues and organs of human body still needs efforts- it is estimated that it will be achieved in 2030-2035. China's stem cell research has been at the forefront of the world. [27:43-40:25]

Reference 中国经济大讲堂- 20200509 健康中国：干细胞如何创造生命奇迹？

Stem cell technology China has used stem cell technology to grow stem cells from urine into teeth. Now, China is studying to use stem cell to make neurons to treat dementia. Stem cell can also be used to develop organs of human body to prolong life.

Reference 开讲了- 20160319 裴端卿：用"万能细胞"延缓衰老是可行的

Other: 中国经济大讲堂- 20200712 我们为什么要探索人脑的奥秘？；
20200503 健康中国：科技创新如何提供助力？；
20190725 如何加强新药研发，打造健康中国？
开讲了- 20190831 当代中国肝胆外科领军者董家鸿院士：医学是人类最大的善意；
北京同仁医院院长王宁利开讲：让世界听到中国眼科的声音；
20170402 大医生开讲健康中国 魏镜；20170311 大医生开讲健康中国 詹启敏；
20170325 大医生开讲健康中国 北京儿童医院院长倪鑫：让儿童医院变成...；
20170318 大医生开讲健康中国 王拥军——为什么要做卓越的医生？；
20200822 本期演讲者：乔杰 test tube baby

IVX. Housing Issues

China's big cities have housing problem, in the following 3 areas: 1. Housing is expensive- the price-to-income ratio, in cities around the world, is generally 2-6, but this ratio in most Chinese cities exceeds this ratio. More than 30 cities have ratios over 10, some over 30. Rent-to-income ratio, in cities around the world, generally does not exceed 30% of monthly income, but most cities in China exceed this percentage, and some are as high as 90%. [2:43-6:25] 2. Difficult to find a house- especially for new citizens, rental ratio of people in an area generally is 67%, the phenomenon of group renting is common, and housing area is small (20 square meters- half of the national average housing area). [6:26-7:46] 3. Poor housing- poor infrastructure: supporting facilities/public services are not complete/ safety risks are high. [7:47-8:13] Harmful effect: micro- affects a family's education/health care/marriage/birth; macro- affects economic growth/scientific and technological innovation/weakens the country's competitiveness/increases financial risk/increases social anxiety contradiction. [8:14-9:00]

China used the following methods to solve its housing problem (1978-2019): 1. Housing commercialization/marketization- it solves housing problem of high-income earners, but not for low- and middle-income earners, 2. In 2007, government-built housing (low-rent housing/public rental housing/provident fund) to solve this problem, and the housing for low- and middle-income people increased from 5% to 30%. [10:48-17:10]

There are now 200 million floating population in China, and the following 3 methods are needed to meet their housing problem: 1. Rent priority- solving housing problem, 2. Combination of renting and selling- buying while renting, solving housing problem in the short-term, and solving housing needs in the long-term, 3. Others: Encourage private rental of excess housing/internet connection between supply and demand. [27:10-41:00]

Reference 中国经济大讲堂- 20210411 租还是买？大城市"蜗居"怎么破？
Other: 中国经济大讲堂- 20191017 揭秘建筑节能

XV. Employment Issue

China has to arrange 15 million people's job every year. Started in 2013, labor force (16-59 years old) in China declined slightly, but employment problem still exists- it is difficult to find a job/employee. This is a structural problem: requirements of company do not match the people seeking employment. China's unemployment rate is 5%; the job demand ratio is 1.28; overall employment is stable. China puts great attention to employment issue- by tax cuts, simplification of procedures, etc. China's economic development is very resilient- talent needs are large, with an increase of 15,000 companies every day. The world is changing, China needs to maintain stability. [1-5:55-20:22]

China's industry is undergoing transformation and upgrading from the primary/secondary industry to the tertiary industry*. Benefits: It is conducive to the employment of college student/will have high-paying career. [1-20:22-31:39] To achieve high-quality employment requires adequate employment opportunities/fair employment environment/good employability/reasonable employment structure/ harmonious labor relations. [1-31:39-40:19]
* The primary industry is food/biological production industry; the secondary industry is processing and manufacturing industry; the tertiary industry is an industry outside the primary/secondary industries such as finance/services, etc. [2]

70% of China's employment is through hiring (80% in developed countries). After 2012, China's economic growth and job creation have become jointly driven by the secondary and tertiary industries. As the labor force declines, the labor supply becomes increasingly tight. But the problem of unemployment still exists, which is caused by a structural contradiction- mismatch in the workplace. China's job-seeking ratio (number of jobs/number of job seekers) has been greater than 1 since 2016, with maximum at 1.6-1.8.

The biggest problem is young people's employment. According to survey, young people's employment will not be stable until after the age of 30. Young people's employment is a worldwide problem, and the average unemployment rate of young people in developed nation is 15%. Long-term unemployment among young people can also cause social problems. Characteristics of Chinese youth unemployment: seasonal- high during graduation/high education level- 15-16 million new labor force per year, 60% is college graduate/young people account for 23.57% of the employed population, 6.2% higher than the developed nation. [3-3:27-21:57]

The current employment problem of young people: number of job seekers is increasing- number of students graduating is increasing, number of oversea return student per year is 600,000-800,000, epidemic hinders study abroad/economic transformation- robots replace people, requiring high technical skill/township youths are not high skill, etc. [21:57-27:40] How to provide high-quality employment for young people: better income/stable job, security/ good working environment/appropriate labor requirement, etc. Key points: create high-quality job/encourage innovation and entrepreneurship. [3-27:40-39:52]

Reference
1. 中国经济大讲堂- 20190801 如何在高质量发展中开拓就业新机遇？
2. 三大产业; https://baike.baidu.com/item/三大产业/7435210
3. 中国经济大讲堂- 20220306 稳中求进关键点：稳就业如何兜牢民生底线？

XVI. Sports

Since 1984, China has participated in 16 Olympic Games and won 286 gold medals, excellent results.

Reference 中国历届奥运会金牌榜;
https://baike.baidu.com/item/中国历届奥运会金牌榜/15683978
Other: 开讲了- 20160827 杨扬：体育让我不再懦弱

Chinese women's volleyball team It won championship in 1981 and 1985 World Cup, 1982 and 1986 World Championship, and 1984 Los Angeles Olympic Game, becoming the world's first "five consecutive championship", and won championship in 2003 World Cup and 2004 Olympic Game, 2015 World Cup, 2016 Olympic Game, and 2019 World Cup, becoming the world champion ten times winner; outstanding achievements.

Reference 1. 中国国家女子排球队;
https://baike.baidu.com/item/中国国家女子排球队/1134805
2. 开讲了- 20161004 本期演讲者：中国女排

XVII. Emergency Management

We live in risk, and we pay attention to the risk event with large loss as follows- small probability (such as air disaster, etc.)/high probability (such as natural disasters, etc.)- gray rhino event/ unknown probability- black swan event. [5:21] China divides major emergencies into 4 categories- natural disaster/production safety accident/public health/social security- which are characterized by high risk and uncertainty. To facilitate response, emergencies are classified according to their severity. There are 4 levels- Level 4 is county level/Level 3 is municipal level/Level 2 is provincial level/Level 1 is national level. [5:28-8:21] The purpose is to reduce the disaster of the event. SARS in 2003 was an important turning point in China's emergency management system- attaching importance to the handling of emergencies. In April 2018, China established the Emergency Management Department to strengthen the handling of emergencies. [13:46-19:41]

The future of handling emergencies: to strengthen prevention/ strengthen institutional mechanisms- coordination, insurance, etc./resilient- improve efficiency/strengthen training. [23:03-41:00]

Reference 中国经济大讲堂- 20200802 如何打造现代化的应急管理系统？
Other: 中国经济大讲堂- 20190328 安全第一，如何守好"不可逾越的红线"？

XVIII. Underground space

China is urbanizing- reached 59% in 2018 and is expected to reach 75% in 2050, 1.2 billion people* need to live in cities and need 50 million mu of land (100 square feet per person- per UN standard). China's land is limited, and currently high-rise buildings are built to solve the problem, but some urban problems have also been found- flooding/pollution/garbage/traffic congestion, etc. [5:00-9:28] China and other countries in the world have begun to use underground space- building city/shopping mall/railroad/sewage treatment plant, etc. underground. [9:28-35:19] Utilizing underground space requires careful planning and safety. [35:19-39:18] * It is estimated that in 2030, China's population will peak at 1.6 billion people.

Reference 中国经济大讲堂- 20190613 地下空间如何助力城市绿色发展？
Other: 开讲了- 20210123 本期演讲者：陈湘生 underground project

IXX. Chinese diplomacy

Since the reform and opening up (1978), China has begun to conduct more diplomatic activities and express more opinions internationally.

Reference 开讲了- 20181222 前联合国副秘书长吴红波：中国外交的时代变迁

XX. Special Achievement

Three Gorges Dam it is on Yangtze River and is the largest hydroelectric power project in the world. Construction began in December 1994 and was completed in May 2006.

Reference 三峡大坝; https://baike.baidu.com/item/三峡大坝/496331
Other: 中国十大水电站排名分布图; https://www.tzixun.com/tzx/4513.html
开讲了- 20200912 本期演讲者：翁永红 Udonde Dam;
20210911 本期分享者：汪志林 Baihetan Dam

Shield machine It is a heavy weapon of great powers. China's first subway, Beijing Line, started construction in 1965 and was completed in 1971, with total length of 10 km and took 4 years and 7 months to finish. Now, with shield machine, it only needs six months to a year to finish. Shield machine is not only fast, but also safe. [4:25-5:36]

China is now in the late stage of industrialization/mid-urbanization, high-speed rail/highway/South-to-North water transfer/West-to-East gas transmission/city pipelines/national defense/water conservancy, etc., all need to excavate many tunnels and need to use shield machine- currently, there are 3,000 shield machines working in China. [5:36-7:30]

Shield machine is a very complex electro-mechanical-hydraulic device. It is a factory that moves underground and completes the procedures of excavation/slagging/lining in a steel drum. It has cutter head/tool/drive and transmission high-power motor/control system/ measurement system; maximum diameter is 17 meters, and one-unit costs more than 500 million yuan. Feature- high cost/knowledge of multiple disciplines/each needs to be custom designed. It also requires the cooperation of skilled construction personnel. [7:30-10:20]

Before 2009, China still needed to import shield machines from abroad. The machines were expensive/having problems/services were poor, so China decided to develop its own shield machine. [10:16-16:37] In 2007, China made the first shield machine, but it was only a year later that it had an opportunity to show its power. After the successful trial, China's shield machine began to sell well at home and abroad. [16:37-35:31] China is continuing to improve its shield machine's manufacturing/operation.

Reference 中国经济大讲堂- 20210103 中国盾构是怎样 "炼" 成的？

Other: 开讲了- 20220305 本期分享者：王杜娟 shield machine

High speed rail China built its first high speed rail in 2008- the Beijing-Tianjin high speed rail (350 km), and by July 2020, China had 36,000 km of high-speed rail. Smart high-speed rail: From 2017 to 2020, China used a new technology- BIM (Building Information Modeling) to develop an autonomous driving smart train, Fuxing. [15:10-17:41] Advantages of China's high-speed rail: safety (no seat belt required)/energy saving and environmental protection- use electricity, less land/large transportation capacity/all-weather operation/comfortable/efficient and fast. [17:41-30:22] China's high-speed rail is low in cost/good in performance/fast in completion and has begun to serve abroad. The future development of China's high-speed rail: faster/intelligent/green. [34:54-41:33]

Reference 中国经济大讲堂- 20201018 为什么中国高铁是一张亮丽的名片？

The history of high-speed rail in China There are 4 stages in the development of high-speed rail in China: 1. Before 2004- started established a team, 2. 2004-2006- research period, high-speed rail speed reached 200 km/hour, 3. 2006-2008- independent research and development period, high-speed rail speed reached 300 km/hour, 4. After 2008, independent innovation period, high-speed rail speed reached 380 km/hour- first in the world. Future- to develop high-speed rail to reach 400 km/hour and to develop maglev train reach a speed of 600 km/hour. [13:30-25:12]

Reference 开讲了- 20180203 复兴号CR400AF动车组总设计师梁建英：中国高铁铺就幸…

Other: 开讲了- 20190727 新京张高铁总体设计师王洪雨：跨越百年的京张铁路

The Longest Tunnel in Central Asia China started the construction of the 20-km Kamchik Tunnel for Uzbekistan in 2013. The work was difficult because there were water surge and rock burst issues. Chinese team took 903 days to complete the project. Opened to traffic in June 2016.

Reference 开讲了-20171022中铁隧道局集团总工程师洪开荣："中国技术" 攻克中亚第一长隧道

Shipping industry Sea shipping is the most economical and convenient means of transportation. There are many types of ships with complex structures and systems. The cost of a ship ranges from tens of millions of US dollars to more than one billion US dollars, so the financial industry and the shipbuilding industry need to be deeply integrated to promote a shipbuilding industry. Shipbuilding industry is a user of various modern technologies. [4:21-11:55]

In 1977, China began to develop a modern shipbuilding industry. After more than 20 years of hard work, China's shipbuilding industry has become the only industry in the world that can independently build various ships. Since 2010, China's new ship construction/ marine equipment manufacturing/ship repair industry is the world's first. [11:55-17:48]

The 3 pearls of China's shipbuilding industry are large LNG carrier/ aircraft carrier/large cruise ship. [17:48-22:58] Innovation in China's shipbuilding industry: using LNG as fuel/boost with airfoil sails/ ballast water management system, etc. [22:58-31:49] The future of China's shipbuilding industry: continuous innovation/green development/cultivating talents/international cooperation. [31:49-40:08]

Reference 中国经济大讲堂- 20220320 船舶工业如何为海洋强国提供装备支撑？

China's port construction technology It leads the world. Shanghai Yangshan Port is the world's most advanced/largest fully automated container terminal- no need for people to work at the port, and highly intelligent/monitoring only. China has also built modern ports for several European and American countries.

Reference 开讲了-20180106 中国交通建设集团总工程师孙子宇：凝心筑梦交通强国

China bridge In October 2018, the Hong Kong-Zhuhai-Macao Bridge opened to traffic (construction started in December 2009); it is 55 km long and is the longest sea-crossing bridge in the world. Bridge is a load-bearing structure* that spans obstacles and consists of some stress-bearing members. There are four types of bridges: suspension bridge- highest spanning capacity/cable-stayed bridge- second best spanning capacity/arch bridge- third best spanning capacity/girder bridge- lowest spanning capacity, but easy to construct/economical. [1-3:53-7:57][2-5:30-6:00]
* Three stress situations of bridge: tension/compression/bending; bridge is the strongest in tensile and compression capacity and the weakest in bending capacity.

In 1957, China built the first Wuhan Bridge across Yangtze River and began to build bridges by herself. Over the past 70 years, China's bridge building history has gone through learning to build bridges-independent exploration-learning to catch up-improving and forging ahead-innovation and leading. In 21st century, China has become the world's No. 1 bridge-building country. Chinese bridges have achieved the world-class standard in bridge leaping capacity, bridge construction technology, materials, and equipment. [1-7:57-35:26] China's bridge-building industry is still working on technologies and material improvement. [1-35:26-40:54]

Reference 1. 中国经济大讲堂- 20220522 硬核基建：屡创奇迹中国桥

2. 开讲了- 20170701 港珠澳大桥总工苏权科：在伶仃洋上打一枚"中国结"

Other: 开讲了- 20210501 本期演讲者：李军堂 Shanghai-Sutong Yangtze River Bridge

Nuclear power plant Advantage: high energy capacity- 1 kg of uranium is equivalent to 2700 tons of coal, in terms of electricity generation; radioactive products can be utilized and processed, basically, its usage is safe. [3:48-11:32]

Nuclear power plant in the world had 3 accidents: Three Mile Island in United States in March 1979/Chernobyl in Soviet Union in April 1986/Fukushima in Japan in March 2011. [11:32-23:18] China started the research and development of nuclear power plant in 1970, and in 2007, China developed her own nuclear power plant design. [23:18-32:39] Prospects for the future: At present, power generation of nuclear power plant is 5% of the national total, which can be increased to improve the instability of wind and photovoltaic power generation. [32:39-41:34]

Reference 中国经济大讲堂-20210725 实现"双碳"目标，核电如何独当一面？

Other: 开讲了- 20201031 本期演讲者：邢继 Hualong-1 nuclear power plant

Ultra-high voltage (UHV) power transmission Advantage: Long-distance power transmission/large capacity/low loss/less land required. Northwest and southwest China have abundant power resources, and the east needs a lot of electricity; so, there is a need for power transmission from west to east. [5:06-16:04]

China has done basic research on UHV power transmission and independently design/manufacture/construction/operation. In the past 20 years, continuous innovation, and improvement, with advanced technology- not only realized the transmission of electricity from the west to the east, the standard of high-voltage power transmission in China has become an international standard. [16:04-41:00]

Reference 中国经济大讲堂- 20220515 硬核基建：西电东送特高压
Other: 开讲了- 20220312 本期分享者：李立涅 ultra-high voltage power transmission

Fuyao Glass Group It was established in 1987. It is the largest automotive glass company in China and the 2nd largest in the world.

Reference 开讲了 - 20181215 福耀玻璃集团创始人董事长曹德旺：为中国人做一片属于自己的...

XXI. Renovation of environment

Changes in Loess Plateau Loess Plateau covers 85% of the land at Yellow River Basin, with an area of 640,000 square km (6.7% of the national area). Before 1950-1960, there were many problems here- heavy wind and sand/frequent floods and droughts/serious soil loss, United Nations investigated Loess Plateau and concluded that it is not suitable for human habitation. But in 2019, plant coverage of this area had reached 63.6%, and here is the world's largest apple orchard, with an area of 1/5 of the world and a yield of 27% of the world. [4:20-9:04]

In the 1950s, China spent 4 years investigating and researching the methods of controlling Loess Plateau- This is what they did: planting grass on hillsides to prevent soil loss/collecting drained soil with trenches, in the 1980s, began to focus on collecting water with trenches, planting grains on top of the trenches/planting fruit trees beside the trenches; in 2000, began to return farmland to forests, resulting now the green waters and mountains of Loess Plateau. [9:04-20:19]

Technology helps Loess Plateau crops have higher production. [20:19-35:01] Loess Plateau needs more talent to maintain/advance its development. [35:01-38:45]

Reference 中国经济大讲堂-20191207 科技兴农：如何让黄土高原变成“绿水青山”？

South-to-North water diversion It is the transfer of water from Yangtze River to the north. It is the largest scale, longest distance, most beneficiary, and widest range project in China. The current route [12:20]: There are two routes- the east route and the middle route. The east route- starting from Yangzhou in Jiangsu and heading north, after passing through Dongping Lake, it is divided into two routes- extending to Tianjin/Jiaodong, with a total length of 1467 km. The east route's elevation is low and relies on pumps to move water. It also uses Beijing-Hangzhou Grand Canal. It was completed in 2013. [13:00-15:28] The middle route- starting from Danjiangkou and going north to Beijing and Tianjin, with a total length of 1432 km. It has the advantage of 100 m elevation difference; water transportation is controlled by sluice gate. It was completed in 2014 [15:28-21:00]. The western route is still under planning.

Benefits of south-to-north water transfer: supply of domestic water/ flood control/convenient transportation/improve environment- protect underground water and expand water area. [21:00-34:00] Future work: follow-up work on the east route and the middle route. Working on the west route- supplying water to Yellow River, making the northwest an oasis. [34:00-40:48]

Reference 1. 中国经济大讲堂- 20220508 硬核基建：南水北调为发展"解渴"
2. https://baike.baidu.com/item/南水北调东线工程/11037025；
https://baike.baidu.com/item/南水北调中线工程/11036981；
https://baike.baidu.com/item/南水北调西线工程/11037021
Other: 开讲了- 20190406 朱炳仁：让千年运河流动起来;
20201128 本期演讲者：钮新强 South-to-North water diversion

XXII. Other

Standards They are the foundation of high-quality technology. They can make production more efficient/higher quality. Before 1981, China did not participate in any international standard activities. China only participated this kind activities after 1981- hosted 1 activity in 1981- hosted 2 in 1990- hosted 13 in 2000- hosted 106 in 2010- hosted 856 in 2020. The purpose of China's transformation is to develop high-quality development- not only the quality of products, but also the quality of business/economy/government/ national development. Only high standards can bring high quality. [3:33-14:57]

After 40 years of hard work, China has become a large manufacturing country in the world, but not a strong one. Mutual recognition of standards is the most effective way to solve this problem, lack of scientific experimental verification capabilities, and shortcomings. [14:57-22:17] The sign of China's high-quality development success is whether it can cultivate a group of world-class enterprises. Standardization is the foundation of global technology governance, and people are the foundation of standardization, so people who understand technetium standards/professionals/foreign languages are needed. [22:17-30:26]

The new trend of standardization: In the past, there were products first, and then there were standards; in the future, there would be standards first, and then there were product. In the future, the governance of a country will also be standardized. Future products will have a carbon footprint logo. In addition, taxes will be collected according to the logo to encourage the purchase of low-carbon products. [30:26-40:49]

Reference 中国经济大讲堂- 20220327 如何让标准化成为高质量发展的抓手？

Chapter 3 National Defense and Military

I. Beidou Navigation System

From 2000 to 2003, China developed the 1st-generation Beidou Navigation System with three satellites, which can complete domestic navigation. In December 2012, the 2nd-generation Beidou Navigation System was completed with 14 satellites. It is able to complete navigation in the Asia Pacific region. [1-12:53-17:50] China's navigation system has many innovative designs and is easy to use. From June 2009 to June 2020, the 3rd-generation Beidou Navigation System was completed with 30 satellites. It is able to navigate around the whole world, and it is the most advanced navigation system in the world. [2]

The significance of Beidou Navigation System- China has her own navigation system to avoid being controlled by others, which is beneficial to the development of many areas- such as agriculture/ aviation/fishing, etc.

Reference 1. 中国经济大讲堂- 20210207 北斗为何是国之重器？
2. 北斗三号全球卫星导航系统;
https://baike.baidu.com/item 北斗三号全球卫星导航系统/52972330
Other: 开讲了- 20200704 本期演讲者：谢军;
20170924 北斗卫星导航系统总设计师杨长风：万物互联，有北斗

II. Eight artificial islands in South China Sea

After 2012, China has created eight artificial islands in South China Sea: Yongxing Island, Meiji Island, Zhubi Island, Yongshu Island, Huayang Island, Nanxun Island, Dongmen Island, and Chigua Island. They have great military strategic value.

Reference 1. 中国在南海有八个填海造出来的人工岛，你都了解吗？;
https://new.qq.com/omn/20220112/20220112A00HUC00.html
2. 美军要在南海建岛？我国修建 "不沉航母"，击碎美军幻想;
https://www.163.com/dy/article/HA4VHJIT05529LG3.html

III. Air Force- China builds her own aircraft.

Military aircraft: In 1957, a jet trainer was built, and in 1958, a supersonic fighter was built. [1] **Civil jet**: 运-10 civil aircraft was designed in 1970 and was completed after 10 years of hard work. [2]

C919 is a large civil aircraft designed by China, which can take 150-170 people. The first flight was completed on May 5, 2017. [3]

Reference 开讲了- 1. 20170715 飞机设计专家顾诵芬：我的飞机设计生涯
2. 20170708 新中国第一代飞机设计师程不时：大国之翼 翱翔天际
3. 20170520 C919首飞机组机长蔡俊：大飞机的梦想

歼-20 stealth fighter It made its maiden flight in 2011. After 6 years of testing, it was officially put into service in 2017. The advantage of a stealth fighter is that radar on the ground cannot detect its presence.

Reference 开讲了-20191026 歼-20隐身战斗机首飞试飞员李刚：刀尖上起舞，这种感觉很爽！

运-20 transport aircraft 运-20 (鲲鹏号) is a large transport aircraft. In January 2013, after 5 years of research and manufacturing, the first flight was successful, and 3 years later, it was put into service; it can be used for airborne operations and disaster relief.

Reference 开讲了- 20161112 运-20总设计师唐长红：为了鲲鹏展翅那一刻

直-10 armed helicopter It was developed in the 1980s and first flew in April 2003. In addition to 直-10, China also has 直-19/直-20 armed helicopters, and the research and development work is still going on.

Reference 1. 武直 10 解决有无问题, 武直 20 补充数量, 中国未来还需重型武直; https://www.163.com/dy/article/HDJQQ0Q405529LG3.html
2. 开讲了- 20161105 直-10武装直升机总设计师吴希明：追求极致的挑战

Amphibious aircraft AG600 (鲲龙号), used for rescue/firefighting. Since 2009, after 9 years of hard work, it was completed.

Reference 开讲了-20190101 "鲲龙" AG600的总设计师黄领才：上天入海 有我 "鲲龙"
Other: 20200808 本期演讲者：赵生

Drone China has been researching drone since 1980s. In 2007, the first drone, 翼龙 I 号, was built. In 2015, 翼龙 II 号 was built- it is an advanced drone and world first in performance.

Reference 开讲了-20171216 "翼龙" 系列无人机总设计师李屹东：创新从来不是浪漫的事

IV. Navy - China builds its own warships.

Chinese nuclear submarine This project was established in 1965, built in 1968, launched in 1970, the nuclear submarine Longmarch-1, officially used in April 1974, and completed deep-sea testing in 1988. Research and development of China's nuclear submarine started from blank, without any help from any country, like many other projects.

Reference 开讲了 - 20161026 "中国核潜艇之父"黄旭华：此生无悔

Aircraft carrier Liaoning aircraft carrier is China's first aircraft carrier, commissioned in September 2012. China now has three aircraft carriers.

Reference 开讲了 - 20170826 辽宁舰舰长刘喆：舰艏行处是长城
Other: 开讲了 - 20170617 国产航母副总师孙光甦：我们的征途是星辰大海; 20170527 歼-15舰载机总设计师孙聪：不突破常规，就不是好设计师

Hainan amphibious assault ship It is a large-scale warship with main function to transport landing troops. It can carry tank/armored vehicle/hovercraft/landing troop for sea-to-land attack.

Reference 开讲了 - 20220226 本期分享者：闫勇军 Hainan amphibious assault ship

Marines It is a rigorously trained troop, and its equipment is modernized from nothing.

Reference 开讲了 - 20201226 本期演讲者：王家权 marines

V. Army

Tank electrical automation China has developed its own tank firing control system and electrical automation.

Reference 开讲了 -20180811 中国著名坦克电气自动化专家、陆军装甲兵学院教授、中国工程…

A report from an explosive expert The level of explosives in a country determines the level of its weapons. China's level of explosives is leading in the world.

Reference 开讲了 - 20180120 国家最高科学技术奖获得者王泽山：国家的需要是我一生的追求

Rocket army It is China's missile force, established in 1959; began in 1963, it has missile equipment.

Reference 开讲了 -20170818 火箭军"东风第一旅"旅长王锡民：导弹阵地有我们坚守的梦想

Anti-missile system China completed tests of anti-missile system in January 2011, January 2013, and June 2022.

Reference 1. 中国国家导弹防御系统;

https://baike.baidu.com/item/中国国家导弹防御系统
2. 开讲了- 20161029 中国反导任务靶场试验系统副总设计师陈德明：坚定是一种力量

VI. Other

Evacuated Chinese nationals from Yemen On March 29, 2015, Chinese naval frigate Linyi docked at Yemen port of Aden, evacuating 122 Chinese citizens and 2 foreign citizens. On March 30, Chinese naval frigate Weifang with 449 Chinese citizens evacuated safely from the port of Hodeidah in western Yemen. On April 2, frigate Linyi evacuated 225 foreign nationals, becoming the first international rescue operation for a Chinese warship to evacuate foreign citizen. On April 6, frigate Linyi left Yemen with 24 Chinese citizens on board.

Reference 也门撤侨; https://baike.baidu.com/item/也门撤侨/17016699

Peacekeeping troop Since 1990, China has provided peacekeeping troop to United Nations. The main task of the troop is to stop conflicts and restore peace. So far, China has dispatched 22,000 peacekeepers, and had 17 casualties. The peacekeeping troops sent by China are mainly for medical, engineering, and other service.

Reference 中国维和部队; https://baike.baidu.com/item/中国维和部队/5904328

Other: 开讲了- 20210109 本期演讲者：李军 parachute test jumper

Chapter 4 Science and Technology

I. Large scientific installation- Sky Eye

In September 2016, Sky Eye was installed in Guizhou Province; with a diameter of 500 meters. It is the world's largest and only astronomical device to detect the universe. It uses advanced technology (radio astronomy) to discover the various peculiar forms of matter in the universe to reveal the origin and principle of celestial bodies- the mystery of the universe. [1-8:58-9:10] New discoveries have been made and are continuing. [1, 2]

Reference
1. 中国经济大讲堂- 20210829 大科学装置："中国天眼"洞见苍穹解天问
2. 开讲了- 20200201 FAST首席科学家——李菂：星空下的守望者

II. Exploration of the micro world

The collider Optical microscope can magnify the sample thousands of times, so that people can observe the invisible things (microscopic world). We need to use electron microscopes to improve the observation ability a thousand times or use acceleration detectors (colliders) to improve 100,000 times the power of observation. The collider can see electron/proton structure. Now, humans have discovered that matter is composed of 12 kinds of particles. In 1989, China had a collider and obtained some research results, and is now developing a next-generation collider. This is basic research that can impact the future of humanity.

Reference 中国经济大讲堂- 20210822 大科学装置：对撞机能为我们撞出什么？

Hashed neutron source project The purpose of this project is to use high-energy protons to hit targets and produce scattering neutron to explore the microstructure of matter. In August 2017, China had its own hashed neutron source with superior performance. So far, it has achieved excellent results. It is also used to treat cancer.

Reference 中国经济大讲堂- 20210808 大科学装置：探索微观世界的"火眼金睛"

III. Artificial sun The official name of artificial sun is magnetic confinement nuclear fusion, which has been studied by human for 60 years. It is the ultimate energy pursued by human because the raw material (heavy water) it uses comes from the ocean, which is inexhaustible and relatively safe; the current raw materials used in power plants- coal/uranium, will be used up one day. However, there are also difficulties in using artificial sun to generate electricity, which need to be overcome by research, and it is expected to be realized in 2050. [1] In 2006, China built the first artificial sun. In 2015, improvements were completed with self-made equipment. There are currently 7 countries/organizations cooperating (including China) to study this project in France. [2]

Reference 1. 中国经济大讲堂-20210516 大科学装置："人造太阳"如何"照亮"未来？
2. 开讲了- 20160416 李建刚：我的"太阳"在中国
Other: 开讲了-20190413 北航物理科学与核能工程学院院长昌广宏：聚变未来，你也可成..

IV. 3D printing Manufacturing technology, according to using the amount of material, is divided into 3 types- equal material technology (traditional casting manufacture)/subtractive technology (manufacturing parts to combine)/additive technology (that is, 3D printing- an innovative/disruptive technology). 3D printing is controlled by a computer, adding material little by little to make product. It saves materials, the product is light, superior, and production time is short. [3:37-5:42]

Advantage of 3D printing: save money and labor in high-end manufacturing/can manufacture complex and precise equipment/simple and fast/no material restrictions; Others: speed up product innovation and research and development/accelerate the research and development iteration of high-end equipment/improve industrial competitiveness. 3D printing is a competitive artifact in high-end manufacturing. [5:42-22:19]

China now has 3D printing technology. [22:19-28:31] 3D printing has been used in medical treatment [28:31-34:58] and will be used in space in the future. [34:58-41:18]

Reference 中国经济大讲堂- 20220213 3D打印如何突破高端制造的瓶颈？
Other: 开讲了-20180616 中国工程院院士、西安交通大学教授卢秉恒：3D打印，让你的...
20200725 本期演讲者：王华明

V. Special material

Super steel In 1996, China became the world's largest steel producer (100 million tons); in 2018, China's steel production (900 million tons) was more than the rest of the world combined. Now, what is to be improved is the quality/efficiency/profit of the steel industry, etc. [4:20-7:06]

Steel becomes high precision/performance/benefit steel during rolling, China has developed super steel manufacturing with its own technology. [7:06-19:55] China's future iron and steel industry will develop in the following 4 aspects: process greening- energy saving and emission reduction/equipment intelligence/product quality/ service. [19:55-40:28]

Reference 中国经济大讲堂- 20200419 材料之光：我们如何打造"超级钢"？

Ceramic matrix composite material In 1970s, France invented silicon carbide ceramic matrix composite material, which will not broken, just like metal; its properties- high temperature resistance/high strength/low density/oxidation resistance/corrosion resistance /weldable. It can be widely used in space/aviation/nuclear power plant/ automotive industries. In 2004, it won the first prize of National Technology Invention Award. Now, it is understudied to be used in other aspects- such as high-speed rail/subway/ship, etc.

Reference 中国经济大讲堂-20201212 材料之光：揭开陶瓷基复合材料神秘的面纱

Carbon fiber It is an amazing man-made fiber- as thin as hair/light as feather/strong as steel/hard to make/expensive as gold. [1-3:30-11:06] Carbon fiber can be used in aerospace/aviation/sports, etc. China began to manufacture carbon fiber by itself in 2004 and has continued to improve [2]; high-performance carbon fibers were produced in February 2016. [3] The future of carbon fiber in China- needs to achieve high quality and low price, expand application, and increase independent innovation. [1-34:34-41:11]

Reference
1. 中国经济大讲堂-20210627 大科学装置：瞄准科技前沿，实现创新突破
2. 中国碳纤维的四十年; https://user.guancha.cn/main/content?id=662988
3. 被西方高度封锁的技术：碳纤维在中国的发展史;
https://baike.baidu.com/tashuo/browse/content?id=ced913fd27ebe516c93805ee

Graphene It is a single layer of graphite, transparent, can withstand a lot of pressure, has good electrical/heat transfer properties, and has the potential to become a useful new material in 21st century. China's graphite production is 65% of the world. [4:08-13:39] Graphene has 3 different forms- powder/film/fiber, with different uses; powder- as an additive/film- for electric heating and health products, etc./fiber- composite product used in airplane, etc; plus many other uses. [13:39-32:08] China's graphene is mainly used in 3 aspects- new energy battery 71%/paint 12%/health 7%. Its application is still under study. [32:08-41:38]

Reference 中国经济大讲堂-20210711 材料之光：神奇的"新材料之王"石墨烯

VI. Lithium battery In 2018, China's lithium battery output ranked first in the world; in 2019, it was 73% of the world. In late 1970s, China began to study lithium batteries, and in 1995 the first lithium battery was manufactured. [4:59-15:22] Lithium batteries are small, easy to use and have many uses, and have become a necessity of life. Lithium batteries can be used as an energy source for electric vehicles, which can reduce CO_2 emission. Its future is in improving safety/improving quality/developing other batteries.

Reference 中国经济大讲堂- 20200229 锂电池如何驱动"电动中国"？

VII. Quantum What is Quantum? Anything obeys quantum mechanics is quantum. Quantum world is an uncertain probabilistic world. What follows traditional mechanics (classical physics such as Newtonian mechanics) is the definite classical world. The classical world is limited, but the technology of quantum world can surpass the classical world. [4:48-14:09]

Quantum devices are an important step for mankind to the quantum world. We are still in the exploratory stage of quantum. The hallmark of quantum age- having practical application by a universal quantum computer; it can help solve many problems that cannot be solved by classical technology. Many countries are working in this area. [14:09-40:28]

Reference 中国经济大讲堂- 20191003 量子技术将如何彻底重构经济生活？

History of quantum science in China Since 1984, there have been achievements in quantum information, and research is still going on.

Reference 开讲了- 20190202 著名量子信息学家、中国科学院院士郭光灿：邂逅神奇的量子世界

VIII. Artificial Intelligence (AI)

AI is the intelligence created by human through the carrier (robot/computer). Two important concepts: strong AI- It is as capable as human or better/weak AI- it can only do one thing.

History of AI: In1956, at Dartmouth, USA, 10 people published an article about artificial intelligence, it started the era of AI. The next 20 years (to 1976) was the first stage of AI development, and the main work was to use computer to simulate human brain in logical reasoning; 1976-2006 is the second stage of AI development, the main work is to use computers to develop expert systems, such as medical/consulting/fault diagnosis/neural networks, etc. After 2006, it is a deep neural network era. By 2015, the error rate had dropped to 3.6% (lower than the human error rate of 5%). [5:21-18:32]

Intelligence is divided into perception (easy)/cognition/decision (difficult). For AI to progress from perception to cognition, brain-like computing and quantum computing are needed- yet to be done, what can be done now is human-machine hybrid intelligence; but the relationship between man and machine needs to be determined. Applications can lead to the development of AI. [18:32-24:57]

China is already one of the AI powers; some technologies, such as face/speech recognition technology, are already at the forefront of the world. In 2017 and 2018, China's AI patents surpassed those of United States and Japan. China's advantages in developing AI: national policies/mass data resources/opportunities to use/many talents. However, China's development of AI also has shortcoming: lack basic theories and original algorithms/lack high-end devices/ lack open platform/lack high-end talents. [24:57-34:17]

AI will promote the 4th industrial revolution, and it will be the core of this revolution, which is estimated to occur in 2030-2040. To develop AI well, planning needs to pay attention to its strategic location/sound R&D system/talent training/strengthening intelligent infrastructure/legal ethics research/deepening international cooperation. [34:17-40:38]

Reference 中国经济大讲堂- 20190808 未来已来，人工智能将如何改变我们的生活？

Internet It will make our lives more convenient- online medical/ shopping/research, etc.

Reference 开讲了- 20200613 本期演讲者：杨善林

The history of internet It began in United States in 1969; China began in 1994. Internet technology innovators must declare to give up intellectual property rights, so they will not get rich.

Reference 开讲了 - 20180127 中国工程院院士清华大学计算机科学与技术系主任吴建平：中国...

5G internet It has already started in China, and the popularity is the first in the world. Advantage of 5G is that it is faster/more function, can do more/difficult work, and promote economic development.

Reference 开讲了 - 20190720 中国工程院院士邬贺铨：5G会如何塑造我们的未来？

Large data Collecting data, analyzing it, can help us understand/solve problems, make our life better and more convenient.

Reference 开讲了 - 20180310 中国科学院院士、北京理工大学副校长梅宏：大数据时代，你准...

Robot China has become the largest market for robot since 2013. Robot can do simple labor as well as complex thinking. The age of robot has come.

Reference 开讲了 - 20160514 曲道奎：机器人的时代到来了

Self-driving car Its advantage is that there is no need for a human to drive, avoid human mistake causing car crash. Since 1989, China started to study self-driving car. From 2015 to 2017, self-driving car have been developed in city and country driving. This technology has been applied to minecart. [1-9:03-19:37] The technology of self-driving car and bus, is still under study. [1-19:37-41:44]

Reference 1. 开讲了 -20160507 中国人工智能学会会长李德毅：期待赛车场上"人机大战"
2. 中国经济大讲堂 - 20210912 自动驾驶离我们还有多远？

Other: 开讲了 - 20200523 中国工程院院士、阿里云创始人王坚：城市大脑是如何从无到有；
20180602 中国工程院首批院士，遥感测绘专家刘先林：让智慧城市"活"...；
20191116 中国科学院外籍院士、北京大学访问讲席教授约翰·霍普克罗夫...

IX. Integrated circuit It is a chip. In 1945, the first computer was built with vacuum tubes. In 1947, transistor was invented- it is smaller and reliable than a vacuum tube. In 1954, a computer was built with transistors. In September 1958, chip of integrated circuits was made. In 1962, IBM built a computer using chips. In 1981, computer for personal use appeared. [2:19-8:56]

Chips keep improving and getting smaller to today. Chip in 2019, is only 7nm*. [8:56-18:39] China is the largest user of chips, accounting for 34% of the world. [18:39-20:32] Chip manufacturing has 3 parts: design/packaging-testing/manufacturing. China is already at the forefront of the world, but it still needs improvement.

[20:32-25:44] Problems in China's chip industry: large gap between industry and demand/lagging development, not enough investment /more innovation needed/insufficient talent. The development of chip still has a long time to go- about 100 years. The development of a chip industry is not easy and requires a lot of investment and long-term persistence. [25:44-39:12] * 1 nanometer = 10^-9 meter.

Reference 中国经济大讲堂- 20190620 高质量发展如何从"芯"突破

Nanotechnology The ratio of a nanometer ball to a ping pong ball is like the ratio of a ping pong ball to earth. China started nanotechnology research in 2001 and is continuing.

Reference 开讲了- 20210605 本期演讲者：赵宇亮 nanometer world
Other: 开讲了- 20220319 本期分享者：赵东元 nanometer drilling

X. Maglev train Unlike high-speed rail, it is suspended on the track, and other different- running mechanism, power, traction, and control system. Advantage of maglev train: less maintenance work- because there is no friction.

In 2002, China had a Sino-German joint venture maglev train, which used German technology, but Germany did not teach their core technology. It took China 20 years to develop its own core technology.

Application of high-speed maglev train: Its speed is 600 km/hour. It is faster than high-speed rail, at 350-400 km/hour and slower than airplane, at 800 km/hour. It can be used for fast transportation within and between metropolises, filling the gap of high-speed rail/aircraft.

Reference 中国经济大讲堂- 20220529 硬核基建：贴地飞行磁悬浮
Other: 开讲了- 20210130 本期演讲者：梁建英 maglev train

XI. Space breeding Seed mutate in the environment of space, and some become new varieties. [3:45-12:20] China started space breeding in 1987. In 2006, China launched a special biological breeding satellite. This is the first in the world. In 2020, deep space breeding was done on Chang'e 5*- this is a milestone work. Advantage of space breeding: high frequency of seed mutation/ shortened breeding cycle/multiple breeding targets/produced large mutations/provided more and better agricultural products and food. [12:20-25:40] * It is a space module landed on moon.

Aerospace breeding has improved the breeding level/became the source of biological breeding innovation/guaranteed national food security. [25:40-35:52] Others: Not all seeds carried by spaceflight will have good mutation. It is safe to screen/space breeding because seeds themselves have changed, and there is no interference from foreign genes. Future space breeding will require a fusion of space technology, biotechnology, and data technology; in addition to cultivating seeds on the ground, seeds in space must also be cultivated. [35:52-41:27]

Reference 中国经济大讲堂- 20210718 解密航天育种

Other: 开讲了- 20201024 本期演讲者：刘录祥 space breeding

XII. Explore deep inside of earth Earth has an outer layer and an inner layer; the outer layer includes atmosphere/biosphere/ hydrosphere, and the inner layer includes crust/mantle/core. Core is the heart of earth, the birthplace of geomagnetic field*, the engine that drives the earth to run. [4:00-11:51]
* Geomagnetic field shields earth from the wind and cosmic rays from universe and sun, protecting living creatures on earth.

In 1970s, humans discovered that there are biological groups that rely on chemical energy to survive on the seafloor of several km; through drilling, it was found that there are microorganisms under the ground several km deep. [11:51-14:57] The temperature of earth makes creatures possible to live; while Venus and Mars near earth, their temperature makes no creatures can survive. [14:57-19:41] The underground minerals/thermal energy is abundant and needs to be further developed. [19:41-24:49] The underground space also needs to be further developed. [24:49-28:53]

China began to explore the deep inside of earth in 2008, and progress has been made and will continue. [28:53-40:51]

Reference 中国经济大讲堂- 20211003 如何与地球谈谈心？

XIII. Other

Supercomputer It is a computer composed of many computers, which is characterized by being able to do a lot of calculations very quickly, so it can solve complex problems. China began to develop supercomputer in 1978; in 2010, it took 7 months to complete China's first supercomputer, and in November, it won the title of world number one. Supercomputer work in China continues.

Reference 开讲了-20171111 十九大代表、超级计算机研发科学家孟祥飞：新时代 以创新...

Gaofen-7 satellite It was launched in November 2019. It is a stereo mapping satellite with spatial resolution of 0.65 meter. It is China's 7th high-resolution satellite; can provide remote sensing information data for mapping (1:10000)/shooting 3D large-scale movie/ inspecting disaster area/observing crops/high-speed railway land-based settlement (saving manpower), etc. China is still improving its high-resolution satellite and providing services to the world.

Reference 开讲了- 20200919 本期演讲者：童旭东 Gaofen-7 satellite

Atomic clock and time Atomic clock can precisely determine time. Different industries have different requirement for the accuracy of time; the aerospace industry requires very precise time.

Reference 开讲了- 20210102 本期演讲者：张首刚 atomic clock/time

Fossil From fossils, we can learn about the past and future life on earth.

Reference 开讲了- 20210424 本期演讲者：沈树忠 fossil

The problem of scientific and technological progress The current problems of China's science and technology: 1. Lack of cutting-edge scientific and technological talents, 2. The integration of science and technology and economy is still not smooth, 3. The confidence in innovation is insufficient. [7:14-16:13] The solution lies in independent innovation; China needs to develop more mid/high-end technologies. [16:13-19:44] Three weak links of Chinese science and technology: 1. Weak original innovation, 2. Weak integration innovation, 3. Weak introduction, digestion, absorption, and re-innovation; need for independent innovation. [19:44-26:05] 5 keys to implementing independent innovation: 1. Pay attention to small people and small projects- give them a chance, 2. Enterprises must become the main body of technological innovation- because they are closer to society, 3. To vigorously support the innovation activities of small/medium enterprise- so that they can develop, 4. Actively participate in international scientific and technological cooperation projects- need international cooperation, 5. To fully understand and play the role of major projects- which can lead the development of other industries- requires taking risks. [26:05-37:56] Several suggestions for building a strong country in science and technology: setting up youth science and technology award/establishing financial support for basic research/implementing the plan to revitalize the entrepreneurial service industry/reforming and implementing scientific research evaluation and reward system/strongly support the popularization of science and technology. [37:56-40:37]

Reference 中国经济大讲堂- 20190905 科技强国梦，我们该如何实现？

Science It is part of culture; some have practical value, some don't. China needs to integrate science into life, not just pay attention to its practical value.

Reference 开讲了- 20160402 王贻芳：科学有什么用？

Other: 中国经济大讲堂- 20200816 材料之光：如何打开神奇的纳米世界？；
20200322 奋斗在科技前沿（上）；20200329 奋斗在科技前沿（下）；
20200222 如何给创新一个机会？；20191215 如何跨越科技成果转化的"死亡之谷"？；
20210801 大科学装置：打造国之重器，迎接新科技革命；
20170422 空间科学部首席科学家张双南：我们为什么缺少科学精神？
开讲了- 20160924 杨培东：科学是从零到一百的探索；
20160910 颜宁：女科学家去哪儿了？；20210313 本期演讲者：孙明月 forging

Chapter 5 Space/Ocean Exploration

I. Explore space

Why do we explore space? Because space has three kinds of resources: 1. Orbital resources- It is a wealth, because it can serve us, 2. Environmental resources- space has no gravity. It can be used to serve us. Solar energy of space is more abundant than it at ground*, 3. Material resources- There may be resources in space that we need, so we need to explore and find out. Now, it has been found that there are minerals on moon that can be used. [4:42-14:07]
* Earth has an atmosphere of 100 km, which greatly weakens the effect of solar energy at ground.

How to use the resources of space

In April 1970, China launched the first satellite into space, becoming a country capable of developing space. Satellite has many uses- such as navigation, communication, etc. China has also established a space station in space, where experiments can be done.

Reference 中国经济大讲堂- 20210110 我们为什么要向太空进发？

China's manned space project

In September 1992, China started its manned spaceflight project; it is a three-step plan- launching manned spacecraft- space laboratory- space station. [1] International Space Station, which refused China to join, began construction in 1998, began operations in 2010, and will cease operations in 2024. [6]

Manned spacecraft In November 1999, China launched the Shenzhou-1 spacecraft, which began the exploration of manned spaceflight. In October 2003, Shenzhou-5 carried China's first astronaut, Yang Liwei, into space. [1] By July 2022, China has made 24 launches of manned space project. [2]

Space laboratory In September 2011, space laboratory Tiangong-1 was successfully launched. Shenzhou-9/Shenzhou-10 carried astronauts to Tiangong-1. In March 2016, Tiangong-1 ceased service. In September 2016, space laboratory Tiangong-2 was successfully launched. Shenzhou-11's astronauts and Tianzhou-1's cargo were delivered to Tiangong-2. In July 2019, Tiangong-2 ceased service. [3, 4]

Chinese space station It has 3 parts: Tianhe core module, and two experimental modules- Wentian experimental module and Mengtian experimental module; and another connector to accept the cargo from Tianzhou spacecraft. In April 2021, Tianhe core module entered space; in June, Shenzhou-12 carried 3 astronauts into the core module. In July 2022, Wentian experimental module docked with the core module. Mengtian experimental module will be docked with the core module in October. The lifespan of Chinese space station is 10 years. [5]

Reference 1. 中国载人航天历史: 中国人的飞天梦, 正在一步步的实现; https://new.qq.com/omn/20210618/20210618A05D9U00.html
2. 中国载人航天; http://www.cmse.gov.cn/fxrw/index.html
3. 天宫一号; https://baike.baidu.com/item/天宫一号/6355172
4. 天宫二号; https://baike.baidu.com/item/天宫二号/2341431
5. 中国空间站; https://baike.baidu.com/item/中国空间站/6287565
6. 国际空间站; https://baike.baidu.com/item/国际空间站/40952
Other: 开讲了- 20170304 中国载人航天工程总设计师周建平：我们为什么要探索太空; 20170225 长二F火箭总设计师张智：一个新总师的心路历程; 20170218 天宫二号总设计师朱枞鹏：造一座梦想的"天宫"; 20160730 杨宏：路虽远，行则将至

Report of the Shenzhou-11 astronaut He lived in space for 33 days. His experience: feeling of floating without gravity, feeding each other, growing vegetables, the experience of returning to earth, etc.

Reference 开讲了-20180512 神舟十一号航天员陈冬开讲：我是航天员陈冬，我想在文昌发射

Long March-11 carrier rocket Feature: sea launch/simple/efficient/ flexible/fast/commercialized. This project was established in 2012, first flew in September 2015, and first launch in June 2018.

Reference 开讲了- 20201121 本期演讲者：彭昆雅 Long March-11 carrier rocket

Dark matter particle detection satellite Wukong Einstein said that 95% of the universe is dark matter and dark energy (invisible, but present), of which dark matter accounts for 27%. Countries all over the world want to know about it because it is a mystery of universe and physics.

China started its research in 1980s; in 1992, put more effort; in 1995, began to study high-energy electrons and gamma rays in the universe. In December 2015, satellite Wukong was launched to collect data from space; two years later, a lot of data was obtained- still understudy.

Reference 开讲了- 20171209 暗物质粒子探测卫星"悟空"首席科学家常进开讲

II. Exploration of moon

China started exploring moon in 2004- the Chang'e project. Chang'e-1 was launched in 2007 to survey the surface of moon at an altitude of 200 km; Chang'e-2 was launched in 2010 to survey the surface of moon at an altitude of 100 km; Chang'e-3 was launched in 2013 to send probes to the surface of moon, facing earth). [3-0:0-17:18]

China's Chang'e-4 landed on back of moon in January 2019, making the first human exploration at back of moon. [1] In December 2020, Chang'e-5 landed on moon and back to earth with lunar soil, which was the first time for human. [2]

The exploration of moon has increased the understanding of moon, and the exploration will continue. Moon has the potential to become a base for human exploration of space. [3-17:18-40:44]

Reference
1. 嫦娥四号; https://baike.baidu.com/item/嫦娥四号/3954372
2. 嫦娥五号; https://baike.baidu.com/item/嫦娥五号/9026516
3. 中国经济大讲堂- 20220501 我们为什么要去月球"挖土"？
Other: 开讲了- 20201205 本期演讲者：吴炜琦 satellite launch center

III. Mars Exploration

Probe Tianwen-1 In July 2020, China launched probe Tianwen-1 to explore Mars. In February 2021, after adjustment, it entered an orbit around Mars and landed on Mars in May. [1] The rover Zhurong came down from Tianwen-1 to conduct Mars exploration. [2]

Reference 开讲了- 1. 20210227 本期演讲者：李海涛 Tianwen-1,
2. 20210724 本期分享者：张荣桥 Mars rover Zhurong

IV. Scientific expedition to ocean

Since 1980, China has been conducting scientific expedition of ocean and has made efforts to understand it.

Reference 开讲了- 20171223 "科学"号首席科学家周慧博士："海洋人"的蓝色情怀

Advance into deep sea Why advance into deep sea? 60% of the earth is sea, and 200 meters below sea surface is a dark world, with various creatures and minerals waiting for us to explore. The average height of land is 800 meters, and the average depth of ocean is 3700 meters. 85% of the world's volcanoes are in sea, and many submarine organisms rely on the heat/minerals emitted from the earth's interior to survive. [6:22-22:02]

Ocean has: 1. Oil and gas- 50% of the world's economy now comes from oil in ocean, 60% of new oil and gas comes from seabed, 2. Minerals- manganese/cobalt/sulfur compounds, rare earth metals, etc., but technologies to fetch them are not yet mature. [22:02-29:26]

There are 3 methods of deep-sea exploration: deep diving- deep into seabed to observe/deep drilling/deep net- establishing a deep-sea exploration network to understand deep sea. China is already doing them. [29:26-37:38]

Reference 中国经济大讲堂- 20201011 我们为什么要挺进深海？

Qianlong-2 It is an underwater autonomous robot that does not require human operation and can complete tasks by itself. Its job is to do resource exploration in the complex deep sea. Qianlong-1's job is to explore flat seabed. Qianlong-3 is about to join the exploration work. Other marine research will also start- achieve six dragons* plus a dragon palace deep sea study. *Existing deep-sea equipment: Jiaolong- manned submersible/Sea Dragon- Remote submersible/ Qianlong- autonomous submersible/Xuelong- Antarctic expedition, there will also be Deep Dragon- drilling at the bottom of the sea/ Kunlong- seabed mining/Cloud Dragon- network under the sea.

The ocean is rich in minerals, more than the land. The International Ocean Organization stipulates that if a country detects resources in a certain sea area and provides relevant data/information, it will have the priority right to exploitation.

Reference 开讲了- 20180331 "潜龙二号"总设计师刘健开讲：我们为什么要探索海洋

Striver manned submersible It is independently designed by China. In November 2020, it dived into the bottom of Mariana Trench at 10,909 meters, setting a world record.

Reference 开讲了- 20210619 本期演讲者：赵洋 Striver manned submersible

Antarctic expedition In December 1984, a Chinese expedition arrived in Antarctica; in February of the following year, a research station was established in Antarctica. [1]

In 1992, China bought the Xuelong-1, and after modification, in 1993, it began to investigate in Antarctica. In October 2019, China's self-built icebreaker Xuelong-2 also went to Antarctica for the 36th expedition. [2]

Reference 开讲了- 1. 20191005 本期演讲者：颜其德;
2. 20200627 本期演讲者：赵炎平

Other: 20190105 中国极地研究中心研究员，中国南极昆仑站首任站长李院生：问…

Chapter 6 Defend the Homeland

China has made many efforts to defend her territory, and even in the early days, when her national strength was weak, she did not back down. We want to review the following pieces of history:

In 1950, China resisted U.S. aggression and aided North Korea. China repelled U.S. military and keep North and South Korea at the 38-latitude line. In June 1962, India invaded Tibet and was repelled by China. In March 1969, Soviet Union invaded Zhenbao Island and was repelled by China. In January 1974, South Vietnam invaded Xisha Islands and was repelled by China. In 1975, after the reunification of Vietnam, Vietnam invaded Guangxi and Yunnan, and in February 1979, China launched a self-defense counterattack. In 1997, Hong Kong was returned to China. In 1999, Macau was returned to China.

I. Resist US aggression and aid Korea

In August 1948, Republic of Korea (South Korea) was established in the southern part of Korean peninsula; in September, Democratic People's Republic of Korea (North Korea) was established in the northern part; they are bounded by the 38-latitude line. Neither side gave up the goal of reunification, and there were armed conflicts near the 38-latitude line, which finally led to the Korean War in June 1950.

In the early days of the war, South Korea was losing ground. At the end of June, United States sent troops to help South Korea and organized a United Nations coalition led by US military to participate in the war. By the end of August, North Korea had reached the 35-latitude line. In September, U.S. troops landed in Inchon, repelling North Korea. China warned U.S. that it would not sit back and watch U.S. troops head north. In October, US military ignored China's warning, crossed the 38-latitude line, and sent planes into China to bomb Dandong. At the same time, North Korea asked China for assistance, and China sent volunteers to help the war, opening the war to Resist US Aggression and Aid Korea.

The first stage of the war is from October 1950 to June 1951. At this stage, Chinese Volunteer Army and North Korean Army conducted five campaigns based on mobile warfare*. Result: Push U.S. forces back south of the 38-latitude line. * Mobile warfare is a tactic, mainly to avoid enemy's main force, lure enemy into depth, and concentrate superior forces to defeat them one by one.

The second stage of the war is from June 1951 to July 1953. At this stage, Chinese and North Korean armies implemented the strategy of "protracted operations-active defense" and took positional warfare as the main form of combat to conduct protracted active defense operations. In July 1951, the two sides of the war began to hold Korean armistice talks. Since then, the war has been fought and discussed for more than two years.

On July 27, 1953, both sides of the war signed the Korean Armistice Agreement. So far, the war to Resist US Aggression and Aid Korea, which lasted 2 years and 9 months, has ended.

Reference 抗美援朝; https://baike.baidu.com/item/抗美援朝/383

II. India invaded Tibet

In 1962, China had just survived a 3-year drought and was in desperate need of peace. Internationally, China was also isolated-falling out with Soviet Union and blockaded by US. In 1959, India started to create disputes on the border and occupied Chinese territory.

In October 1962, India launched an attack on China at the border, which lasted 28 days; the Indian army was defeated- the 7th Brigade of the Indian Army was wiped out in the eastern section, and the Indian army invading the Galwan Valley and Red Hill was wiped out in the western section. China did not want to expand the war and ordered its troop to stop pursuing forward.

India regarded China's truce as weakness, launched an anti-China movement at home, and persecuted overseas Chinese. On November 14, India launched a second attack on China. China defeated the Indian army again, and recaptured all areas north of Jimo Mountain Pass, pushing the front to the traditional boundary between China and India. However, due to national conditions, China issued a ceasefire order again on November 21, and the troops also took the initiative to retreat. China treated Indian prisoners kindly and returned all captured weapons- this is a rare thing in the world.

Reference 1962 年中国举目皆敌, 印度意图侵占西藏, 被我军歼灭四千

III. Zhenbao Island self-defense counterattack

The Sino-Soviet border issue has always been an unsolved case. In the early days of the founding of China, Sino-Soviet relations were close, and the border issue was shelved. However, in late 1950s, Chinese and Soviet parties had differences on policy. In 1959, Soviet Union favored India on Sino-Indian border issue, and suddenly withdrew all experts and suspended all aid construction projects. The shelved border issue was raised again.

Beginning in 1964, Soviet Union successively increased its troops to Sino-Soviet border areas and continued to create incidents on the border. From October 1964 to March 1969, the number of border incidents provoked by Soviet Union reached 4,189, an increase of one and a half times compared with the period from 1960 to 1964. The border disputes mainly focus on the ownership of Zhenbao Island and Qiliqin Island. In January 1966, Soviet Union and Mongolia signed a 20-year military alliance to increase the threat to China. Soviet Union had millions of soldiers on the northern border of China, which remained unchanged from the mid-1960s to the early 1980s.

On March 2, 1969, Soviet border guards dispatched more than 70 people and took 4 military vehicles to invade from the upper and lower reaches of Zhenbao Island and attacked Chinese border guards, killing and injuring 6 people. Chinese border guards counterattacked in self-defense and drove the invading Soviet troops from Zhenbao Island. On the 15th, the Soviet border guards dispatched more than 50 tanks, armored vehicles, and more than 100 infantry three times to launch a fierce attack on Chinese border guards with the support of helicopters and artillery fire, and bombarded areas within China with a variety of artillery. Chinese border guards fought fiercely for nearly 9 hours, withstood 6 sharp artillery attacks by the Soviet and thwarted the attack. On the 17th, Soviet border guards dispatched more than 70 infantrymen to invade the Island with the support of tanks. Chinese border guards repelled it with artillery fire and defended the country's territory.

After the Zhenbao Island incident, Sino-Soviet negotiation began. Because Soviet Union did not recognize the disputed border between

China and Soviet Union. Negotiation failed to make progress. Since July 1978, negotiation on the Sino-Soviet border issue have been in adjournment status.

After the Zhenbao Island Incident, Soviet Union had a new evaluation of China's strength, which stopped Soviet Union's war attempt. Since then, the attitude of both China and Russia have changed. With the end of the Cold War and the disintegration of Soviet Union, China and Russia continued to deepen their ties and became strategic partners, which not only promoted the sound development of bilateral relations, but also played a positive role in the peace of Northeast Asia.

In 2004, China and Russia also reached an agreement on Heixiazi Island. Russia will return to China all the occupied Yinlong Island, part of the territory of Heixiazi Island, and Abagaitu Zhouzhu on the Ergun River near Manzhouli, Inner Mongolia.

In March 2005, China ratified the agreement; in April, Russian also ratified the agreement. So far, not only has the territorial dispute over Heixiazi Island settled, but the 4,300 km border between China and Russia has also been confirmed.

Reference 珍宝岛自卫反击战;
https://baike.baidu.com/item/珍宝岛自卫反击战/1222207

IV. South Vietnam invaded Xisha Islands

In August 1973, South Vietnam began to occupy China's Xisha Islands, despite China's protest. At that time, the strength of Chinese navy was weak, but in January 1974, four frigates from the East China Sea Fleet were dispatched to pass through Taiwan Strait and arrived at Xisha Islands, where they joined the local patrolling navy.

In the 4-day battle of Xisha, South Vietnamese navy dispatched 4 destroyers and gunboats with a total tonnage of more than 6,000 tons, while Chinese navy dispatched 4 frigates and 2 hunting submarines. The total tonnage was only 1,600 tons.

Chinese Navy adopted a close-range combat strategy, defeating South Vietnamese Navy; one South Vietnamese warship was sunk, and two Chinese warships were severely damaged. Chinese Army took Ganquan Island, Jinyin Island, and Shanhu Island; more than 50 South Vietnamese soldiers were captured on the islands.

Reference 1. 1974 年东海舰队驰援西沙;
https://www.163.com/dy/article/HDQ9HQ9L055271PN.html
2. 南越入侵西沙群岛视频;
https://cpu.baidu.com/pc/1022/275122716/detail/111841200244/video

V. Self-defense counterattack against Vietnam

This battle, in a narrow sense, refers to the war between China and Vietnam from February 17 to March 16, 1979. In a broad sense, it refers to the nearly ten years border military conflict from 1979 to 1989.

In July 1976, after the unification, Vietnam considered China as the number one enemy. The Sino-Vietnamese relation deteriorated. Vietnamese army violated China's territory, and the stability of Chinese frontier and the lives and property of people were seriously threatened. Under such circumstances, on February 17, 1979, China retaliated against Vietnam in self-defense. On March 16, all Chinese troop returned to China. The campaign disrupted the strategic deployment of Soviet Union and Vietnam, destroyed the industry and mining facility in northern Vietnam, protecting China's territorial integrity and peace in Southeast Asia.

In 1981, China recovered Koulin Mountain and Faka Mountain, and in 1984 China recovered Laoshan Mountain, Zheyin Mountain, and Balihedong Mountain. Through the ten years of Sino-Vietnamese border war, the stability of southwest of China was maintained, and Vietnam's national strength was consumed and destroyed for a long time.

Reference 对越自卫反击战;
https://baike.baidu.com/item/对越自卫反击战/946798

VI. The Return of Hong Kong

On July 1, 1997, Hong Kong returned to China.

In June 1840, in the first Opium War, Qing government was defeated and ceded Hong Kong Island and Ap Lei Chau to Britain. From October 1856 to October 1860, in the Second Opium War, Qing government was defeated, and the south of Boundary Street and Stonecutters Island on the Kowloon Peninsula were handed over to British. In 1898, Qing government signed a contract with Britain to lease 230 large and small islands to the south of Shenzhen River and north of Boundary Street, with a total area of 975.1 square km to British. The leased land was called New Territories, and the lease term was 99 years.

In September 1982, China and Britain began negotiating on future issues of Hong Kong. After two years and 22 rounds of negotiation, China and Britain finally signed the Sino-British Joint Declaration on December 19, 1984, deciding that from July 1, 1997, China would establish a special administrative region in Hong Kong and begin to exercise sovereignty.

Reference 香港回归; https://baike.baidu.com/item/香港回归/1287541

VII. The Return of Macau

On December 20, 1999, Macau was returned to China.

After the Opium War in 1840, Qing government was defeated. Portugal took this opportunity to occupy Macau Peninsula, Taipa Island, and Coloane Island after 1849. In 1874, the Portuguese broke into Xiangshan Zhuxin Gate, and took this as the boundary of Macau without authorization. In December 1887, Qing government signed a contract with the Kingdom of Portugal, confirming that Portugal could be permanently stationed in Macau. Since then, Portugal has occupied Macau for more than 100 years.

In May 1985, Portuguese President was invited to visit China to conduct friendly consultation with China on the settlement of Macau issue. The two sides decided to negotiate Macau issue in Beijing in the first half of 1986. In June 1986, China and Portugal held the first round of talk on Macau issue in Beijing.

On April 13, 1987, China and Portugal signed a contract, declaring that Macau is China's territory. On December 20, 1999, China and Portugal held a power handover ceremony at the Macao Cultural Center, and China resumed the exercise of sovereignty over Macao.

Reference 澳门回归; https://baike.baidu.com/item/澳门回归/1058256

VIII. The Taiwan issue

In 1949, when New China was established, only Taiwan was still under the control of Kuomintang. In 1950, when the Korean War broke out, United States intervened to protect Taiwan, and it has been this situation until now.

In 1945, when Taiwan is returned to China, 300,000 Japanese were naturalized and stayed in Taiwan. In 1949, many Chinese from mainland came to settle in Taiwan. The people in Taiwan today consists of the native (descendant of early mainland immigrant)-majority, new immigrant (descendant of mainland immigrant after 1945) and naturalized Japanese descendants.

When Kuomintang ruled Taiwan, the 228 Incident broke out, which caused the natives to be hostile/unfriendly to the new immigrants, some natives began to seek Taiwan independence, and the descendants of Japanese immigrants were also making waves. After the death of Chiang's father and son, Taiwan regime fell into the hands of a half-Japanese, Lee Teng-hui, who strengthened relations with United States and Japan and hostile to China. In September 1986, Democratic Progressive Party (DPP) was established, advocating Taiwan independence- it uses the local relationships to win support of natives and political power.

From 2000 to 2008, Chen Shui-bian of DPP was in power, and he was later jailed for fraud. From 2008 to 2016, Kuomintang's Ma Jiuying was in power and improved relations with China. In 2016 - now, DPP's Tsai Ing-wen is in power, the anti-China campaign continues, and launched de-Sinicization policy- not allowing schools to teach Chinese history and culture. DPP does not put the interests of people first, but only pays attention to gain political power and personal interests.

In August 2022, DPP invited the speaker of U.S. Congress to visit Taiwan to help local election, disregarded China's strong opposition. After the visit, China began to conduct 3-4 days of live-fire exercises in seven water areas around Taiwan, blocking Taiwan. This exercise shows that China has the ability to take over Taiwan by force. On August 10, China issued a white paper of Taiwan: Repeat its decision to take over Taiwan and unify China, and mentioned that after Taiwan is recovered, a one country-two systems can be implemented in Taiwan.

Taiwan is the result of China's 14-year fighting against Japan, and Taiwan independence will never be allowed.

Reference 民主进步党; https://baike.baidu.com/item/民主进步党/1991650

Chapter 7 Outlook of China's Future

Over the past 40 years after China's reform and opening up, China has made great efforts to build and improve, from being poor and backward to becoming prosperous and advanced, creating a rare miracle in the world. China's progress will continue. China's success is because of its good policies- reform and opening up/democratic centralization, hard work, and having talents. What is valuable is that after China became strong, it did not colonize/invade surrounding countries like the imperialist countries in the 19th and 20th centuries but based on an equal footing with other countries in the world, helping to build, mutual benefit, and promoting world peace.

The question is how long China's progress will last. History tells us that a country will thrive for a period and then declines, without exception. The reason is that people are mentally weak. When they are poor, they will strive to improve, but when they are rich, they or their offspring will enjoy and indulging, going downward. For a country to continue to prosper, it must know how to guide the country and its people to continue the right path. The methods are the rule of law, education, and knowing the God in Bible.

Knowing the God in Bible can help a person live a meaningful life, loving one's neighbor as oneself, and being righteous, something the rule of law and education cannot help.

9 798845 972521